RONA MUNRO

Rona was born in Aberdeen and is currently Senior Playwriting Fellow for the Traverse. Credits for the Traverse include: *Iron, Fugue, Your Turn to Clean the Stair*, and a version of Evelyne de la Chenelière's *Strawberries in January*. Other theatre credits include Lorca's *The House of Bernarda Alba* (in a version for Shared Experience); *Snake* (Hampstead Theatre); *The Maiden Stone* (Hampstead Theatre & Royal Lyceum Theatre, Edinburgh; Peggy Ramsay Memorial Award Winner); *Gilt* (co-writer); *Bold Girls* (Susan Smith Blackburn Award, Evening Standard Most Promising Playwright Award, Play International Award, Critics Circle and Plays and Players Most Promising Playwright Award); *Saturday Night at the Commodore* (7:84); *The Way to Go Home* (Paines Plough/Royal Court); *Piper's Cave* (Paines Plough Workshop & Boilerhouse); *Long Time Dead* (Paines Plough/Drum Theatre Plymouth); and adaptations of *Mary Barton* (for Manchester Royal Exchange) and *Watership Down* (for Lyric Hammersmith). Film credits include *Ladybird Ladybird* (directed by Ken Loach, Film Four/Parallax Pictures Ltd); *Aimee and Jaguar* (Senator Film Production). For television, recent credits include *Rehab* (BBC2); *Almost Adult* (Channel 4). Radio credits include *Citizens* (BBC Radio 4); *The Dirt Under The Carpet* (BBC); *Watching Waiters* (BBC); and *Kilbreck* (BBC Radio Scotland).

Rona Munro

THE INDIAN BOY

NICK HERN BOOKS

London

www.nickhernbooks.co.uk

A Nick Hern Book

The Indian Boy first published in Great Britain as a paperback
original in 2006 by Nick Hern Books Limited, 14 Larden Road,
London W3 7ST

The Indian Boy copyright © 2006 Rona Munro

Rona Munro has asserted her right to be identified as
the author of this work

Cover photograph by Clare Park
Cover design by Ned Hoste, 2H

Typeset by Country Setting, Kingsdown, Kent CT14 8ES
Printed and bound in Great Britain by Biddles, King's Lynn

A CIP catalogue record for this book is available from
the British Library

ISBN-13   978 1 85459 973 5
ISBN-10   1 85459 973 9

The Indian Boy was first performed by the Royal Shakespeare Company at The Cube in the Royal Shakespeare Theatre, Stratford-upon-Avon, on 7 November 2006, with the following cast:

JUNE	Holly Aird
NURSE	Claire Catchart
PETER	Christopher Fulford
SPARKS	Ryan Gage
BRICKS	David Kennedy
SARA	Ashely Madekwe
JULIUS	Colin Salmon
INDIAN BOY	Rhik Samadder
CHIPPY	Roderick Smith

Director   Rebecca Gatward
Designer   Liz Cooke
Lighting   Craig Sheppard
Sound score   Matt McKenzie
Movement   Liz Ranken

THE INDIAN BOY

Rona Munro

Characters

INDIAN BOY / ADIL, *fifteen*

BRICKS, *workman, thirties*

SPARKS, *workman, early twenties*

CHIPPY, *workman, fifties*

PETER, *hard one to call, thirties to sixties*

JULIUS, *psychologist, late thirties, forty*

NURSE, *thirties*

JUNE, *late thirties, forty*

SARA, *nearly fifteen*

ACT ONE

A wood / building site. Summer.

Birdsong, green leaves, sunlight, a beautiful forest glade, an ancient oak tree. There is a half-built house nearby.

The INDIAN BOY *is standing at the edge of the trees. He is barefoot. He is wearing ancient finery, so faded it's almost transparent. His hair is very long. He is looking up into the branches.*

He imitates the sound of a bird, a chaffinch.

He talks quietly, rapidly, to himself. To no one at all.

INDIAN BOY. Rain. Rain. Rain.

So you say. So you say.

She does it all. She does it all and you just watch. Wood and feather and good wool. She makes a shell so you can be the kernel, sweet inside. She does it all and you watch and shout the weather. Rain. Rain.

No wood above my head. Rain's a crown, rain's a crown on my head, my crown.

The bird stops singing for a moment. The INDIAN BOY *takes a deep breath, scenting the air.*

He searches for grubs on the underside of leaves and eats them as he climbs the tree.

My teeth shall have you before you are hard. My teeth shall have you and you shall never fly. Never fly now.

He is halfway up the tree now, looking around as he eats.

Nothing eats me but I eat all I see. I wear the rain in my eyes and on my skin.

He leans on the tree a moment, stroking it.

Older than me, will always be. Older than me, will always be. Older . . . Older . . .

He sees the building work through the trees. He leans towards it, scenting the air again.

(*Growing uncertain.*) Always . . . Always.

A sound, a cement-mixer maybe.

(*Muttering, more agitated.*) They took the skin off the earth. They took the skin off the trees. (*Sniffing.*) Earth with no skin. Trees with no skin.

I don't know. I don't know.

Earth with no skin. Trees with no skin.

I don't know. I don't know.

Rain. Rain.

A rustling roar as wind blows through the treetops. The INDIAN BOY *clings to the branches, looking up at the sky. He howls back at the wind.*

He moves further into the tree until he is just visible through the branches.

Time has passed.

BRICKS, SPARKS *and* CHIPPY *are walking through the site to start work. They look around.*

SPARKS. Where is everyone?

CHIPPY. This isn't good.

SPARKS. Where are they?

BRICKS. Hang on, hang on, it's early yet, they could be . . .

SPARKS (*interrupting*). It's because of what happened to the digger, isn't it?

BRICKS. This isn't funny any more.

CHIPPY *notices the* INDIAN BOY *in the tree first, then* SPARKS.

CHIPPY. Look.

SPARKS. Woah!

BRICKS. What? What's the problem? (*Sees the* INDIAN BOY.) Shit!

The INDIAN BOY *doesn't move.*

SPARKS. Is he . . . ?

BRICKS. What?

SPARKS. I mean . . .

BRICKS. What?

SPARKS. We're all seeing that, aren't we?

Pause.

CHIPPY. Yeah.

No, he's there, look. He's . . . not a ghost.

You can see him breathing.

BRICKS (*scornfully*). Ghost!? It's just a kid. (*As they don't reply.*) It's just a kid mucking about, for Christ's sake! Chuck a bit of two-by-two at him! (*Shouting up at the INDIAN BOY.*) Come on! Get out of it! Come on!

SPARKS. Oy! Get out of it, go on! Condemned timber! Condemned timber. Get out of there!

CHIPPY (*to BRICKS and SPARKS*). Stop it!

The INDIAN BOY *slips out of sight, into the leaves.*

BRICKS (*shaky, covering*). There you go. There you go. Job done.

SPARKS. He's still in there. Somewhere. Isn't he?

BRICKS. No.

Pause. None of them move to investigate.

SPARKS. Well, this is the last potato that splits the sack, isn't it?

BRICKS. What are you on about?

SPARKS. After everything else that's happened? I'm not going down there. I'm off home.

SPARKS *starts to move off.*

BRICKS. Oh, are you going to tell him? Are you?

SPARKS. No. I won't be here, will I? My absence will speak for itself, won't it?

BRICKS. You think I'm going to tell him?

SPARKS. You think you can work with that staring at you . . . ?

He points to where the INDIAN BOY *was.*

BRICKS. He's gone!

CHIPPY. He's still in there. We all know that.

BRICKS. He's run off home!

SPARKS. So let's see you start work.

Pause.

BRICKS. Haven't had a cup of tea yet.

He sits down, turning his back on the woods. Taking out his flask.

SPARKS. See, you won't go in there either, will you?

BRICKS. Haven't had my breakfast! I want to raise my blood sugar. If it's all right with you. If the sight of me swallowing tea isn't too terrifying for you.

SPARKS. Thing is . . .

What they're saying . . . What I heard was . . .

BRICKS. What?

SPARKS. These woods are cursed.

BRICKS. Cursed!

You'll be cursed when the boss gets here. We all will.

CHIPPY. They're not cursed!

BRICKS. See!

CHIPPY. Haunted maybe. Not cursed.

BRICKS *has got his phone out and is talking into it.*

BRICKS. Jez? Pick up . . . pick up . . . pick up . . . !

SPARKS. What do you mean, 'haunted'?

CHIPPY. Just . . .

BRICKS. If you're lying there nursing the flu then I'm the tooth fairy. Get down the Peaswood site with the crew, now! Boss is on his way.

CHIPPY. People have seen things. In the trees.

SPARKS. What things?

BRICKS. They better be seeing five ugly blokes and a lorry load of topsoil pretty soon or there'll be all kinds of trouble.

CHIPPY. A boy.

SPARKS. A boy? Like . . .

He points up at tree.

BRICKS. No.

CHIPPY. Yes. My grandparents saw him once, when they were courting.

It was a special memory for them. They were in love.

Grandma said they watched him for five, ten minutes. He moved through the trees, he bent over the stream and drank like a deer.

Pause.

BRICKS. Yeah but, point is, she didn't see this toerag, did she? Be sensible.

CHIPPY. How do you know? That's what I'm saying.

They say if you've seen him it means the woods are awake.

BRICKS. And the hills are alive with the sound of music. haha

CHIPPY. They say one time a bride on her wedding day went wandering in the trees picking bluebells. Then later, at the reception, she says she can hear music when the band's not even started up, dances out the hall straight under a milk tanker. Another time, the postman says he sees someone watching him through the trees, follows them, shouting and throwing stones, walks right over a twenty-foot drop . . .

BRICKS. What postman?

CHIPPY. I don't know his name.

BRICKS. When was that?

CHIPPY. I don't know. Nineteen thirty-something.

BRICKS. Nineteen thirty? You're making that up!

SPARKS. I just heard the woods were cursed. I never heard any of that stuff.

BRICKS. What woods? Where are they? We've had them all, haven't we? Felled. Mud and stacks of two-by-fours so chuck one after Caspar the friendly little gobshite and let's get moving.

SPARKS. You get moving!

BRICKS. I'm busy. I'm having my tea.

Sparks. Sparky boy. Come and have a cup of tea.

SPARKS *hesitates.*

Come and have a cup of tea, sit down and stop filling your Pampers.

SPARKS *joins* BRICKS. *He accepts a drink of tea.* CHIPPY *is moving very slowly towards the tree.*

SPARKS. Don't tell me this whole thing hasn't got you spooked too.

BRICKS. A kid up a tree?

SPARKS. No, what happened to the digger?

BRICKS. So it hit some subsidence.

SPARKS. It'd all been surveyed.

BRICKS. And obviously they messed up!

SPARKS. The ground ate it.

BRICKS. You know your trouble?

SPARKS. What?

BRICKS. Low blood sugar. Drink your tea.

CHIPPY. True love.

BRICKS. What about it?

CHIPPY. You can find it here. So they say. Madness or true love. Could be the same thing, of course.

BRICKS. I have never met a carpenter who talks such a pile of rancid chips. 'True love'? You call that conversation? (*To* SPARKS.) Talk about something else. Ignore him.

SPARKS. I don't believe in it.

BRICKS. What?

SPARKS. True . . .

BRICKS (*cutting him off*). Oh, give me a break!

CHIPPY. Hear that? He's whistling at us. Like a bird . . . I can see his face . . .

BRICKS. I get enough of this at home, all right? When I'm at work I expect certain things, bit of banter, cup of tea, sensible conversation. I get enough of this crap at home!

SPARKS. Susan still upset?

BRICKS. Oh, it's a permanent poxy condition with her.

Still she's got some excuse. She's stuck in with the baby, isn't she? Stir crazy. Brain rotting in front of daytime TV.

SPARKS. 'I married my fiancée's twin sister by mistake.'

BRICKS. Did you?

SPARKS. No! Daytime telly.

BRICKS. Yeah, that's the ones.

Thing is, she's not getting out enough. Wants me to bring the world to her. I've got enough on my plate bringing her a wage, can't bring her a life as well, can I? Be reasonable.

SPARKS. 'He cheated on me with chatline babe.'

BRICKS. 'Did you meet anyone I know?' Couples, that's what she means. 'How are they getting on?'

I don't want to know. I wouldn't ask. Relationships are on or off and everything in between is no more interesting than the pattern on the sole of my boot.

SPARKS. 'My years of hell with anorexic pastry cook.'

That was an interesting one, actually.

CHIPPY. He's still watching us.

BRICKS. It's like an obsession for her. If I do tell her some couple has broken up, it'll upset her. She doesn't like it. Puts her in a mood. She takes to drinking vodka and tonic and snarling if I try and get the TV remote away from her.

Why?

SPARKS. I would lie. Let her think the world's full of true love. Why not?

CHIPPY *edges forward.*

BRICKS. She's talking rubbish now. I'm telling you. 'I'd be better off moving back in with my sister.' 'You don't understand me any more.'

She's right. I don't.

There is a sudden clapping of wings. CHIPPY *jumps back.* SPARKS *and* BRICKS *startle, spilling tea.*

CHIPPY. Just a bird! Just a bird!

BRICKS. Sit down! Get your arse on this bit of wood now or I'll spill your sugarless blood all over my bricks.

CHIPPY. I'm all right.

BRICKS. You're seeing ghosts. You're frightening the electricians. You are not all right.

CHIPPY. It was a collared dove. (*Turning to* BRICKS.) There were two collared doves at the edge of the wood there, do you remember?

BRICKS. What?

CHIPPY. Pale grey, pink birds, like . . . faded china.

BRICKS. Birds?

CHIPPY (*pointing*). I reckon that's one of them. See that mess of feathers?

Fox got him when he was pecking at the ground I should think. (*Looking after bird.*) But she's still waiting for him in the tree. They mate for life, collared doves.

BRICKS. If my fists had feathers would that get your attention?

CHIPPY (*searching, picking it up*). They say if you pick a dove's feather from the ground, this ground, you'll have true love all your life. That's another granny tale. (*He offers* BRICKS *a feather.*) Can't hurt.

BRICKS. I don't know what you were doing in the seventies, mate, but my bet is it was way beyond magic mushrooms.

The INDIAN BOY *emerges suddenly from the leaves, close above them and stares down at them.* BRICKS *yelps in fright. As suddenly as he appeared the* INDIAN BOY *vanishes.*

For a moment the workmen are frozen, then they all get up together and move even further away from the tree.

All right, he's still in there.

SPARKS. I'm not going in there.

BRICKS. Why not?

SPARKS. Why not? Did you see him disappear? Tell me that wasn't a pigging ghost.

They all stand, indecisive for a moment.

None of them notice PETER *arriving. His approach is brisk and energetic: ready to start work. He slows to a disappointed halt as he sees them all standing idle.*

CHIPPY. What should we do?

SPARKS. I told you. I'm getting out of this.

BRICKS. Can't just walk.

SPARKS. Why not?

BRICKS. Think he'll pay you if you're not here?

CHIPPY. All right, suppose you're right. It's not a ghost? It's a real kid? We have to do something then, don't we? We have to . . .

He trails off, looking back at the tree.

PETER. Start work?

The workmen all startle.

Just an idea.

BRICKS. I was keeping them happy for you, boss. I was keeping them steady till . . .

PETER. What's today?

CHIPPY. Wednesday.

PETER. Correct, but not the answer I'm looking for.

BRICKS. The twenty-sixth.

PETER. You don't lose a point but we're still looking.

SPARKS. The day the showhouse was supposed to be wired up.

PETER. Bing! We have a winner! And plumbed in and hopefully with four intact, waterproof, weatherproof walls, one of those added extras potential buyers will so appreciate come November!

BRICKS. We eh . . . we saw something, boss.

PETER *looks past them and up into the tree. He is instantly on the alert.*

PETER. Oh yeah? What might that be?

BRICKS. Well . . . it was this kid . . .

PETER. A kid.

SPARKS. It was a pigging ghost.

PETER. A ghost?

CHIPPY. They call him the spirit of the forest. Don't they?

Pause.

PETER. They might. I've got more sense.

But you don't. Is that what we're discovering here?

So you saw some kid swinging through the treetops. You see, I think most people, if they were alarmed at all, would be thinking: 'Why is that boy playing Tarzan at his age, why isn't he down the bus shelter discovering crack with his peer group?' But no. You're worried about whether he's going to suck your soul out your ears and leave you mad enough to dance a jig into the traffic.

CHIPPY (*to others*). I told you. Right under a milk tanker.

PETER. Why is that? Does that make sense to you? What's the matter with you?

SPARKS. It's . . . disconcerting.

PETER. OK, look at the woods, then look at me.

The three workmen obediently look from one to the other.

Now, which do you actually find more disconcerting at this precise moment?

The three answer in chorus.

BRICKS, SPARKS *and* CHIPPY. The woods.

PETER. I see.

Well . . . there are foxes in there. They have been rumoured to nibble toddlers' toes in neglected prams. There are potentially tubercular badgers in there. There are great, jagged-winged rooks that'll crap in your eye and fly off laughing about it. But if we're talking about real risk – and I assume we are talking about genuine risk, I assume three great hulking men in big boots and hard hats are not sitting here, quaking like effeminate jelly because they're scared of stories . . . If we are considering genuine, quantifiable risk then there are stinging nettles in there that'd do you more damage. There are large caterpillars that would provide a better excuse for an attack of the vapours. There are wood spiders with more bi . . .

SPARKS (*interrupting*). I don't like spiders either.

PETER. I don't expect they like you much. Ignore each other and everything'll be fine.

Where's everyone else?

The workmen look at each other.

BRICKS. It was that business with the digger, boss . . . Jez . . . some of the lads felt a bit . . .

PETER. It's an epidemic. Just you three, then? All right. You can finish off and you can have their bonus.

They don't move.

Look, I pay your wages and I have a heavy brow, a threatening eye. (*To* SPARKS.) Don't you think I've got a heavy brow and a threatening eye?

SPARKS (*no idea what's the right answer*). Eh . . .

PETER. Are you intimidated?

SPARKS (*uncertain*). I've no complaints, Pete. None.

PETER. Well . . . So much for worldly authority.

He slumps, apparently defeated. The workmen look at each other.

I'm getting too old for this.

BRICKS. Come on, you're not old.

CHIPPY. My dad worked for him.

PETER. What? I know. (*Looking down at himself.*) It's not clean living. If I knew what the answer was I'd bottle it.

I'll take care of it. I'll shift him.

The workmen look at each other hesitantly.

CHIPPY. Maybe he needs help.

PETER. I'll help him.

The workmen look at each other. Awkward. For a moment no one says anything.

I'll fix it. There's nothing to worry about.

The workmen still hesitate.

You say you've seen a kid in there. I'll investigate. I'll take appropriate action. You can leave it with me.

He claps his hands.

Come on! Jump to it! That's my house you're working on there. My house. My little dream home in the forest. What do you think the bonus will be like on my house?

The workmen start to move off.

(*Quietly.*) Bricks, you hang on a minute.

BRICKS *hangs back.*

You scared too?

BRICKS. Well . . . You didn't see him, boss, he just . . . popped out . . .

PETER. I've seen him. I know. It's a real kid, Bricks. Got to be.

BRICKS. Right.

PETER. But he's trouble. He's delay. He's police and ambulance and more paperwork.

BRICKS. But couldn't we just call . . . ?

PETER. Once he's out of the tree. We need him out of there, fast. No time for ladders and care workers.

BRICKS. I don't see why we can't just . . .

PETER (*cutting in*). I want him shifted now, Bricks.

BRICKS. Right.

PETER. Hold out your hand. Let's see if it's shaking.

Slowly BRICKS *holds out his hand.*

Ooh, little tremor there. Let's see if this fixes it.

He puts a wad of bills in BRICK's *upturned palm. They both look at them.*

Steady as a rock.

BRICKS. All right, you're the boss.

PETER. Just hang back until I need you.

BRICKS *stands back as* PETER *approaches the* INDIAN BOY *in the tree.* BRICKS *picks up a bit of two-by-four.*

I see you. I see you. Time to come out.

Come on. Climb down.

The INDIAN BOY *appears in the branches. He watches* PETER *intently.*

If you don't, the sky will fall, I promise, light will split your head open and let the moths out of your brain. I can do that. (*Change of tone, cajoling.*) Hey, this is me talking. You listening? Course you are. Come here. Come on, you don't want to sit up there. Come down here.

The INDIAN BOY *starts to climb out of the tree.*

That's it. Down you come.

The INDIAN BOY *is out of the tree.* PETER *turns and looks at* BRICKS. BRICKS *steps forward, hefting his stick of wood.*

Blackout.

In the darkness the INDIAN BOY *screams.*

A hospital.

The INDIAN BOY *lies semi-conscious in a hospital bed.*
PETER *is close beside him. He strokes the* INDIAN BOY*'s
battered head.*

PETER. Next of kin.

Who was your daddy, little scrap? Where are his old bones,
eh? No idea have you, darling?

No next of kin. Just me. I've got salvage rights. I found
you. I shook the tree and caught you when you fell out.
(PETER*'s voice is dreamy, hypnotic, drifting out of himself
as he talks.*) There comes a time when everyone has to
move on. That's what I'd like you to understand. You had to
move out of the forest. I have to make a few hundred grand
creating a community of twenty-five executive homes, with
artisan crafted woodwork and remote-controlled garage
doors.

It's about being part of the world.

We all need to learn to be part of the world, darling.

You were in the way. We have to find you another place to
be. I'm not brave enough to send you straight to your grave.
I can send you on the way. It'll be easier for you than it ever
was for me . . . (*Stroking the* INDIAN BOY*'s head in
rhythm with his words.*) You need a house, don't you? You
need a roof over your head. A nice safe little nursery. Clean
and white. Soft sheets. No hard edges for you to toddle into
and trip and break your crown. Swept and scrubbed clean of
germs. They'll cut your nails and tease out all the happy
families living in your hair. You'll smell of powders and
creams and you'll have your own potty.

You need a new daddy. Someone to smile with pride when
you put one stick on top of another or trace the letters of
your name. He'll be a good man. He'll pat your head and

give you jelly babies. You'll like jelly babies, they're good, like grubs dipped in honey.

You need a new mummy. Someone who'll fight to keep you close. Keep you safe. She'll have a lap that smells of honey suckle. You can lay your head there and feel loved for ever.

You need a woman. You need a wife. Someone to turn your head inside out and set you whistling like a starling.

PETER *does a quiet wolf whistle. The* INDIAN BOY *jerks, drifting closer to full consciousness.* PETER *grins.*

You'll hurt when she's hurting and all you'll want in the world is to fix any broken thing she brings you. And you'll go wherever she takes your hand and leads you, like a bullock trotting happily towards the smell of fresh steak. Someone to butcher your youth and lead you dozing and happy under candlewick bedspreads and into the lighting fixtures aisle at the B and Q summer sale.

And then you need a grave. A wooden box. Roses on the lid. A flash of fire and then dark earth under the green trees, sifted white under the moss and tucked up for ever and ever. Part of the world.

PETER*'s voice has grown even slower and more soothing. The* INDIAN BOY*'s eyes shut. He is asleep.*

PETER *has talked himself into a trance state.*

JULIUS *enters.* PETER *doesn't even notice.*

JULIUS. Can I ask what you're doing here?

PETER *starts.*

PETER. Oh! Sorry . . . sorry I was . . . miles away . . .

JULIUS. Are you all right?

PETER. Yes, I just . . . Must have dozed off.

(*Focuses on* JULIUS.) You're a new one.

JULIUS (*offering hand*). Dr James.

PETER (*shaking*). Peter Fellowes.

JULIUS. Oh, you're the man . . .

PETER. I found him. Yes.

JULIUS. I see.

PETER. He hasn't got anyone looking in on him, has he? No family anyone's found. I just wanted to keep an eye. You know. Felt a sense of responsibility. Just want to see him settled all right.

JULIUS (*already checking notes*). Yes, that's fine.

PETER. So what's happening?

JULIUS (*checking* BOY*'s chart*). We're transferring him.

PETER. Where to?

JULIUS. To the psychiatric unit. My unit.

PETER. I see.

JULIUS. There's nothing more anyone can do for him here. Physically, he's healing well . . .

PETER. Will you keep him?

JULIUS. That's impossible to predict at this stage. Early days.

PETER. Can I visit him there?

JULIUS. That's not entirely straightforward. You're not family.

PETER. No, he hasn't got family. (*Catches himself.*) I don't think.

Pause.

JULIUS. If you're not a relative, he would have to ask to see you. I don't think he can give informed consent. I'm sorry. I'm sure you understand.

PETER. You're going to be deciding things for him now?

JULIUS. Legally, I have to make the decisions a guardian would make.

PETER. You a married man?

JULIUS (*surprised by the question*). Eh . . . yes, I am.

PETER. Kids?

JULIUS. A daughter.

PETER. Good. (*Explaining.*) It's just I just think family is important. If you're going to understand a boy his age.

JULIUS. Why do you want to see him?

PETER. I found him. Wouldn't you?

JULIUS. Yes. I'm sure I would.

PETER. And you can decide if it's all right for me to visit?

JULIUS. Yes.

PETER. So, can I see him?

JULIUS. You would have to apply to the unit, in writing –
we'd have to do a few background checks.

PETER. That's all right. I've got no secrets. None I can
remember anyway.

JULIUS. You're building that new development out at
Peaswood, aren't you?

PETER. That's me.

JULIUS. I heard that's near where they found him.

PETER. You been out there?

JULIUS. No, but eh . . . I have been thinking of taking a look.
There was a thing in the Sunday property section, wasn't
there? It sounded like an interesting development. Very
sensitively done.

PETER (*smooth change of gear*). Let me get you a brochure.

PETER *fetches a brochure from his briefcase and spreads it
out in front of* JULIUS.

It's actually a gated development but the beauty of it is
you'd never know. You have all the amenities – pool, club,
private golf – but from the houses themselves you can't see
another building. It's the landscaping, very clever design.

JULIUS (*looking*). Nice. I might make a trip out there.

PETER. Only a forty-minute commute from your desk.

JULIUS. How'd you get planning permission to build down
there?

PETER. Ah . . . Local knowledge. There are the foundations of
a charcoal burners' workings onsite. So it counts as ancient
habitation not woodland.

JULIUS. I just think I might need to move sooner rather than later.

PETER. Family getting big? Everyone's bumping into each other and getting ratty about it?

JULIUS. Something like that.

PETER. These are perfect family homes. Something for everyone. First units available within months, superior units this time next year. I'm putting my own name on one of those.

JULIUS. So you're a local man?

PETER. Never lived anywhere else.

Everyone knows me. Ask anyone round here. I'm the local boy made better than anyone thinks a thieving Gyppo has any right to make it.

Pause. PETER *touches the* INDIAN BOY, *gently.*

No one took me in.

Now I'm building in the gentleman farmers' back yards and who's got the last laugh when I own all the access roads?

The INDIAN BOY *stirs.* PETER *backs off, realises he's revealing too much.*

Oh, listen to me. Lie down and you'll have to charge me a ton just for talking to you. I could take you out there myself if you like. Two birds with one shot. I show you the development, you get to know me a bit better. Then . . . maybe I could check on the boy.

JULIUS (*re the* INDIAN BOY). He's awake.

PETER *reaches into his pocket and pulls out a bag.*

PETER. Try him with one of these.

JULIUS. What are they?

PETER. Jelly babies.

JULIUS. You've been giving him sweets?

PETER. No. But I bet you could.

Just got a feeling about it. (*Grins.*) Call it local knowledge.

Dubiously, JULIUS *takes a jelly baby. He approaches the* INDIAN BOY.

The INDIAN BOY *stays motionless. Wide-eyed.*

JULIUS *offers him the sweet. He moves it closer to the* INDIAN BOY*'s mouth.*

Abruptly the INDIAN BOY*'s head darts forward and he takes it.*

JULIUS (*charmed*). Good for you.

PETER. There you are. He's on his way now.

A room in a psychiatric hospital – winter.

JULIUS *is assembling a camera. He points it at the* INDIAN BOY.

The INDIAN BOY *sits on the floor at one side of the room, looking up at the window.*

His hair has been cut and he is wearing hospital clothes. The NURSE *is wiring him up to machines, attaching electrodes to his skull. He is rocking in quiet distress. Breathing as if frightened. The* NURSE *is gentle but firm. He bats at the wires on his head. She restrains his hands.*

NURSE. I'm sorry, doctor, I thought he was in a good mood today.

JULIUS just watches, he's already making his decision.

The NURSE *succeeds in getting the* INDIAN BOY *to suffer all the wires.*

She kneels in front of him, trying to get eye contact. The INDIAN BOY *resolutely avoids this. He shrinks into himself, motionless.*

The NURSE *looks at* JULIUS, *uncertain.*

Shall I try anyway?

JULIUS *doesn't reply, still thinking. The* NURSE *claps her hands. The* INDIAN BOY *turns his head sharply to look at the sound. He looks at the* NURSE*'s hands, not her face. The* NURSE *claps her hands again. The* INDIAN BOY *looks again.*

That's a good boy.

She claps her hands again. The INDIAN BOY *does not look. She claps again, and again. The* INDIAN BOY *still does not look.*

JULIUS. All right. Stop.

The NURSE *looks at him, waiting.*

Take the equipment away.

NURSE. All of it?

JULIUS. All of it.

The NURSE *starts to detach the sensors, casting uncertain looks at* JULIUS. JULIUS *just stands, looking at the* INDIAN BOY.

NURSE. Dr Frank has a session booked for this afternoon.

Professor Simpson is visiting with his postgrads.

JULIUS. I'll talk to them.

NURSE. But will you want to see him tomorrow?

JULIUS. No.

No, that's enough. He's had enough. He's a puzzle but we'll leave him in peace.

NURSE. Good. I think you're right.

JULIUS *looks at her in surprise, then he smiles.*

(*Defensive.*) Sorry . . . Just, don't like seeing him poked about.

JULIUS. No. Nor do I.

The NURSE *takes the equipment out.* JULIUS *kneels beside the* INDIAN BOY. *He offers a jelly baby. He holds it close by the* INDIAN BOY*'s face. The* INDIAN BOY *snaps it without making eye contact.* JULIUS *laughs.*

It's all right. It's all right. You can keep your secrets.

Keep all your secrets. I'll still keep you safe.

I'll look after you.

The INDIAN BOY *does not react. After a moment* JULIUS *gathers up his own equipment and leaves.*

Same room in a psychiatric hospital – spring.

JUNE *crouches at one side of the room. The* INDIAN BOY *is still looking at the window above him.*

He is looking at the treetops he can see out of the window, mesmerised by their movement.

JUNE. Can you hear me? Hullo?

Pause, waiting for reaction, nothing.

Hullo?

Still nothing.

My name is June. I'm going to sit with you for a while, all right?

Nothing.

There's the sound of rushing wind outside, a tree tossing in the wind, wind rustling and roaring through its leaves.

The INDIAN BOY *starts to laugh in delight. On his feet, staring in delight at the tossing branches. The sunlight hits his face. He stands, head back, as if he's drinking in the sunlight, laughing quietly.*

JUNE *stands up, really shaken.*

Oh!

She moves towards him. As soon as she steps towards him, the INDIAN BOY *wheels to face her, flattening himself defensively against the wall. His face closes down. He is blank and motionless.*

I'm sorry. I'm sorry.

She backs off and sits back where she was.

Look. Look, it's OK. I'm staying here.

He doesn't move. Doesn't take his eyes off her.

The NURSE *enters and stands looking at them. She's carrying a branch from a hawthorn bush. She is about three months pregnant.*

NURSE. Have you seen all the patients you need?

JUNE. Yes, thank you. I . . . I think I scared him.

NURSE. It's easily done some days. Change in the weather can make him very moody. Mowgli, Mowgli, come on, baby . . . (*She makes a chooking noise as if soothing chickens.*) Come on, sweetheart . . .

No, we've lost him.

JUNE. What did you call him?

NURSE. Mowgli. (*Defensive.*) Well, no one knows his proper name, do they?

Little Indian kid lived in the forest. Haven't you seen the film? My kids loved that film.

Tries some more chooking, no response. She takes the branch she's carrying and puts it down in front of the INDIAN BOY. *He doesn't move.*

There you go, Mowgli. You want to pick it up? A present, for you. Pick it up? No?

No movement at all from the INDIAN BOY.

He likes leaves. Anything growing. If he finds any bugs on that he'll eat them.

JUNE. He eats insects?

NURSE. He does. We had a terrible falling out about that, didn't we, Mowgli? That was a bad day. He bit me.

JUNE. Is he violent?

NURSE. Hardly ever these days. We had him on a benzodiazepine but Dr James stopped that a while ago. No need. He's quiet. But he's not really what you're after, is he?

She sees JUNE's *state.*

Are you all right?

JUNE. Yes . . . yes, I just . . . He's the boy they found in the woods last year?

NURSE. Yes. No one knows where he came from.

JUNE *is still looking at the* INDIAN BOY, *mesmerised.*

JUNE. How long will he stay like that?

NURSE. Longest he's ever done is two days. Thirty-eight hours to be exact. That was after they cut his hair. Stood against the wall day and night. Pissed himself where he stood. That's what he thought about haircuts. He doesn't mind now. He's used to it.

He likes having his head stroked, actually.

JUNE. He lets you touch him?

NURSE. Oh yeah. If he's in the mood.

JUNE. Could I see you touch him just now?

NURSE. No, he's definitely not in the mood just now. He's not sure about you.

He was in a bad way when he first came in. Someone had beaten him black and blue.

JUNE. So have they established how much of this is head injuries . . . ?

NURSE. And how much is how he was anyway?

I think this is him. That's what I think. But what do I know? I'm only telling you 'cause you're asking. You won't find that opinion on his chart.

He didn't know what a toilet was, or a bed, or to expect glass in the windows. He banged his face a few times like a bird flying into the pane. But he knew how to dress himself and he knew what a spoon and a knife was . . . Forks . . . forks were a mystery for a while, he'd eat with the wrong end sometimes. He doesn't mind the sound of cars but he doesn't like the telly on loud. He knew what a blanket was. He still sleeps on the floor.

Dr James doesn't believe in forcing patients into routines they can't engage with. Mowgli's quite happy most of the time. As long as he gets a look at the sky.

After a moment the INDIAN BOY *slowly turns back to the window. In a few moments he is rapt, watching the treetops again.*

There now. He's all right.

JUNE. He likes to look out.

NURSE. When the leaves appeared on the branches last week he danced like that all day.

Pause. They stay still looking at the INDIAN BOY. *He is swaying.*

Do you feel it yet?

JUNE. What?

NURSE (*dreamy*). Like you're sitting in the sun smelling new grass with nothing to do all day but watch the birds fly over you. (*As* JUNE *says nothing.*) Whoops. Just me then.

JUNE. No, that's . . . that's what I feel.

NURSE. When he's peaceful this is a very peaceful place to be.

He got me pregnant, you know. (*Seeing* JUNE*'s startled expression.*) Oh, not like that. I blame him, though.

I've got four. I've got one trying to pull the shirt off my back every time she sees me because she can't believe I actually expect her to eat solid food and not my tits. I've got one at the other end that wants the shirt off my back to get her new boots and MP3s. And two in the middle that cover every shirt I've got with mud and spit and baked-bean battles. I was going to have my tubes tied. Booked in.

Then I started to spend an hour a day keeping an eye on Mowgli, just sitting watching him watching the leaves. And I started to imagine what it would be like. I imagined sunbathing on a little lawn, growing a summer baby. I thought about watching it push out my belly as the sunflowers climbed up the side of the house and the swallows dived round the roof. I dreamed of making daisy chains and talking to my tummy in the garden while the other kids were safe inside with three sets of XBox controls and no arguments.

And I thought about that sweet pain that splits you open like a shell and makes a life. I thought about the tug of gums on you, soothing as lazy sex, sitting with my back to the bark of an apple tree watching the sun and leaves make freckles of light all over that tiny, sleepy, sucking face.

And here I am, swelling like flour and yeast and warm water.

JUNE. That's a lovely dream.

NURSE. Isn't it?

Only trouble is we've no garden, no apple tree, no place for a geranium in a pot, let alone sunflowers. My kids wouldn't know what to say if they weren't shouting at each other and the long range weather forecast says it's going to rain all summer.

I was conned.

Never mind. I don't blame you, Mowgli darling, do I? I can still come here and sit with you and have the dream.

JUNE. Does he ever go out?

NURSE. You couldn't take him out. One whiff of the wind. One glimpse of the grass . . . Schoom! (*Makes speed escape noise.*) He's off! You can't take him out unless you drug him till he can hardly walk or put him on a lead, and he'd bite through the lead.

We don't want to do that to him.

JUNE. How old is he?

NURSE. We don't know for sure . . . Fourteen, fifteen . . . He might be older. But he's not developing.

JUNE. Isn't he?

NURSE. No. Might be part of his problem. He's just stuck being who he is.

Pause. JUNE *watches the* INDIAN BOY. *He's swaying slightly now, mimicking the movement of the branches. The* NURSE *sighs.*

Well . . . that's my summer holiday over for the day.

The NURSE *gets ready to leave.*

JUNE. I think he'll be the main focus of my study.

NURSE (*uncertain*). Oh, OK. It's just I was told you only wanted access to the catatonic patients.

Pause.

JUNE. I'll get Dr James to authorise access for me.

NURSE. Yeah, I'd need that. He doesn't have many visitors. Dr James stopped the academic team bothering him. (*Laughs.*) Ooh that was a set to, that was. They didn't like that.

The builder who found him's looked in a couple of times since but that's it.

As JUNE *stays:*

You want five more minutes with him, don't you? I always do.

JUNE. Could I . . . ?

NURSE (*laughs*). Yeah all right, just this once. I've got to go round the other rooms anyway, I'll pick you up in five.

The NURSE *exits.*

JUNE *is settled very comfortable and relaxed now, watching the* INDIAN BOY.

She gives a deep contented sigh. Thinking. She smiles to herself.

JUNE. Will Dr James give me access?

She takes a mirror out of her purse and examines her make-up. She retouches her lipstick.

She takes out a perfume spray and wafts it all over.

The INDIAN BOY*'s head snaps round. He looks at her.* JUNE *checks her make-up again then puts it away. She notices the* INDIAN BOY *watching her.*

(*Surprised.*) Hullo.

Slowly but without hesitation the INDIAN BOY *moves towards her. He lies down and places his head in her lap.*

JUNE *is stunned for a moment then, tentative at first, she starts to stroke his head.*

Hullo. Hullo darling. Do you like this? Do you want me to stay here?

I'll stay here. I'll stay as long as you like.

The sound of wind surging through leaves.

JULIUS*'s office.*

JUNE *is talking to* JULIUS. SARA *sits in a waiting area outside, absorbed in her homework.*

Under the following scene PETER *enters and watches the* INDIAN BOY.

JUNE. I should thank you.

JULIUS. For what?

JUNE. For giving me this chance.

JULIUS. You don't have to thank me for that.

JUNE. Well . . . I want to.

JULIUS. I think you're very talented. I always have.

Pause.

So . . . tell me. There are some promising options for your study there, aren't there?

JUNE. Everyone was very helpful.

JULIUS. Good.

Pause.

JUNE. It's really impressive, how you deal with such a range of patients.

JULIUS (*interrupting*). June? What is it?

JUNE. What do you mean?

He just looks at her.

I'm nervous, Julius, give me a break!

JULIUS. Don't be. Don't be nervous. It's just me.

JUNE. Exactly.

I haven't been on a ward for a while. Lot of memories . . .

JULIUS. Of course.

JUNE. There was this one patient who really shook me up.

They call him Mowgli down there?

Pause.

JULIUS. That would be Patient Ajay.

They're calling him Mowgli?

JUNE. Yes.

JULIUS. Well, that's completely unacceptable. Thank you. I'll investigate that.

JUNE. Oh, but she seems . . . They seem very fond of him.

JULIUS. Hardly the point.

JUNE. I remember you talking about him . . . But when I saw him . . .

JULIUS. Something about Ajay provokes a very strong reaction. I know.

JUNE. He's *wild*, isn't he? There's something in his eyes and the thing is, Julius, I remembered . . .

JULIUS (*cutting in*). He's not catatonic.

JUNE. No, but he made me remember . . .

JULIUS (*interrupting again*). The proposal you submitted was for a study on reactions to stimuli in long term catatonic patients.

JUNE. Can't you just tell me a little about him?

JULIUS. Why do you want to know?

JUNE *says nothing.*

Everyone wants to know about Ajay. Is he a 'wild child'? Has he been living in the forest, talking to the animals? Has he been running with packs of wild dogs like those kids in Russia?

JUNE. Don't get angry.

JULIUS. Why did those kids do that? Because their home environment was unsafe, violent, they were suffering abuse. They were abused kids who became street kids. We don't need to attach some romantic notion of she-wolves suckling babies to a story like that, and if you want my honest opinion, I find the idea quite offensive.

What can he tell us about language development? He can tell us that a child who's been through all that may never speak.

Pause.

Sorry.

Maybe I should talk to you another time.

JULIUS. Now, come on. We can do this.

Pause.

JULIUS. How's Sara?

JUNE. You know how Sara is. You saw her on Tuesday.

JULIUS. I meant, how do you think she is?

JUNE. Well, how does it go again, oh yeah . . . (*She's quoting* JULIUS.) 'I shouldn't be a conduit in your relationship. It's far healthier if you make your own judgements on Sara now.'

Pause.

I brought her. She's waiting outside. If you've got time . . . ?

JULIUS. I'll make time.

JUNE. She won a prize. For poetry.

JULIUS. She told me. And that science mark . . .

JUNE. She wants to drop science for A Level. She wants to talk to you about that.

JULIUS. Well, I don't think that's a good idea.

JUNE (*cutting in*). Well, it's up to her, isn't it?

PETER *leaves the* INDIAN BOY*'s room. He comes to the waiting area outside. He sees* SARA. *He watches her, speculative.*

She looks up at him. He smiles. She goes back to her books.

JULIUS *and* JUNE*'s dialogue runs over this action.*

JULIUS. June. Ajay's a difficult subject for me to talk about.

JUNE. Why?

You can't work him out, can you?

JULIUS. 'Work him out', is that a technical term?

JUNE. You know what I mean.

JULIUS. I know if you're not precise with your language, you're unlikely to be precise in your thinking.

JUNE *laughs.*

What?

JUNE. God, Jules, if you could hear yourself . . . (*Checks herself.*) All right, I'm sorry. Give me a moment here.

JULIUS *waits.*

PETER *is reading* SARA*'s work. She looks up, annoyed.*

PETER (*pointing at her work*). Wolves.

SARA. What?

PETER. Wolves.

SARA. What about them?

PETER. They mate for life, you know. Completely wild but they mate for life. Nice idea, isn't it?

SARA *just stares at him.*

Don't mind me. Just something to think about.

He smiles at her and turns away. He moves to wards JULIUS*'s office, listening.*

JUNE. Tell me why it's so wrong to work with this boy.

JULIUS. He's a complicated case. There are too many unknowns. We have absolutely no idea what environment would be familiar to him. For instance, he could have been abandoned by illegal immigrants as the child who was too

problematic to integrate into the new life. There could be
cultural complications that we'll never come close to
guessing.

PETER *is hearing all of this.*

JUNE. Yes, but when I saw him – I felt something. I felt . . .

JULIUS (*interrupting*). You can't construct a thesis out of one
isolated . . .

JUNE (*interrupting*). All I was trying to do was tell you what I
was feeling!

JULIUS. We don't know his story. We can't know his story. I
could crack him open to see what was broken, but if I can't
put him back together again that's just meddling for the
sake of getting my name on a few publications.

JUNE. No, you can't do that.

JULIUS. And I didn't!

I know what he needs. He needs peace. He needs to feel
safe. He needs to be left alone.

PETER (*in the door*). He needs a mum.

They turn and look at him.

Stands to reason. It's not rocket science, is it?

And, while we're spelling out the obvious . . . Marital strife –
what a lot of work that makes for the world, all your friends,
all your family, lawyers, therapists . . . You're mugs, the pair
of you. All you're making is grief for the good and gold for
the greedy. Get a grip, go on, kiss and make up.

Pause.

JUNE. Who's this?

JULIUS. Peter Fellowes. I'm buying a house from him . . .

JUNE. Right.

PETER. Ideal family home . . .

JUNE. So this is how I discover you're moving out permanently,
is it?

Pause.

PETER. Julius. I'm really disappointed in you.

JULIUS (*to* JUNE). I'm sorry. He wasn't supposed to be here till . . .

JUNE (*cutting in*). I like him.

PETER. Course you do.

JUNE. When did you two first meet? When did you start window shopping for new houses, Julius?

PETER. Oh, I found the boy.

JUNE. Last year.

PETER. That's right.

JUNE (*still looking at* JULIUS). When we were still talking about getting mediation?

JULIUS (*quietly, just to* JUNE). June, don't do this. We *agreed* . . . we agreed we should separate. It was a *mutual* decision, you know it . . .

JUNE. Could you ring down to the staff nurse and authorise my access?

JULIUS. June . . .

JUNE. Could you ring down to the staff nurse and authorise my access?

JULIUS. Of course.

He picks up the phone.

PETER. Storm in an acorn cup.

JULIUS. Hi, it's Dr James . . . Can you sort out a keycard and badge for Mrs James? . . . Yes I'll sign on it then. Thank you.

Puts phone down.

You can pick that up on your way out.

Pause.

JUNE. Thanks. All right, I'll get stuck into brainwave patterns in the long-term catatonic. Sara's got swimming at six. I'll tell her you'll see her at the car.

She leaves the office. SARA *looks up.*

Wait in the car, Sara, I'll be five more minutes.

SARA. But Dad . . .

JUNE. He'll see you at the car. Five minutes, Sara. We're running late.

JUNE exits. SARA *sighs heavily and gathers up her books. She exits close behind* JUNE.

PETER. Do you want me to fix that for you?

Pause, as JULIUS *ignores this and fights for self-control.*

I can fix that for you. That's all I'm saying.

JULIUS (*tightly*). Really?

PETER. Without a doubt. What would you say the problem was? (*As* JULIUS *still doesn't answer.*) Roughly, just a broad outline. Has the magic gone?

JULIUS. *What!?*

PETER. Don't try and hit me, Julius, you'd never connect, I'm quicksilver.

He feints in demonstration.

JULIUS. What do you want, Mr Fellowes?

PETER. Peter. Can't backtrack on intimacy, Julius. I came to see the boy.

JULIUS. You don't have to come to me every time. The staff nurse knows . . .

PETER (*interrupting*). Been there, done that, bit disappointed.

JULIUS. Excuse me?

PETER. Not progressing, is he?

Pause.

JULIUS. Well . . . we've all been disappointed by that. Now if you don't mind . . .

PETER (*cutting in*). I blame you, Julius. Sorry, but I do.

JULIUS. Really.

PETER. I trusted you with his life.

JULIUS. I didn't realise it was in your gift.

Pause.

PETER. All right, as a favour, if you don't grudge me one, spell it out for me. What's wrong with him? What are you doing to fix him?

JULIUS. In layman's terms . . .

PETER. Oh, please . . .

JULIUS. He's suffered prolonged emotional damage, probably permanent damage, which means he can't relate to others in any meaningful way.

PETER. He's forgotten how to be human.

JULIUS. If you like.

PETER. Sure he's not just putting it on because they're cunning little weasels at that age . . . ?

JULIUS (*cutting in*). He's very damaged.

PETER. Right.

And what are you doing about it?

JULIUS. Everything we can.

PETER. You've given it your best shot?

JULIUS. He's completely unresponsive.

PETER. Yeah, but he knows what you're saying to him.

JULIUS. No.

PETER. Yeah, but he knew . . .

Stops himself.

JULIUS. What?

PETER. Nothing.

JULIUS. He knew what you were saying to him?

PETER. No.

Pause. PETER *is very troubled, recovers. He throws some paperwork on the table.*

Provisional title deeds, have your lawyer take a look. You're
a big disappointment to me, Julius, but the boy needs you.
We won't write you off just yet. I'll fix things for you, no,
don't thank me, glad to do it.

PETER *exits.*

INDIAN BOY*'s room.*

JUNE *approaches the* INDIAN BOY*'s room. The* INDIAN
BOY *moves again. He picks up the hawthorn branch and looks
at it carefully, turning it to and fro.*

INDIAN BOY (*quietly*). Red face . . . red face . . . red face . . .
(*He tries to push his face into the leaves.*) Can't, not like
you, red face, caught like you red face, caught but never
sing, caught but never sing . . .

Red face can put his nose in thorns, right in, I put my nose
in thorns I'm red face too . . .

Caught but never sing. Caught but never sing. Kill you or
let you go. Kill you or let you go.

JUNE *is right outside the* INDIAN BOY*'s room.*

*He's instantly silent, head cocked as though he's listening to
her presence, aware of her but not looking at her.*

JUNE *enters the sealed unit. The* INDIAN BOY *starts to
rock again, he makes breathy whispering nonsense noises,
no words but exactly in the rhythm of words.*

JUNE *sits down and watches him. After a moment the*
INDIAN BOY *comes over and lays his head in her lap again.*

PETER *stands in the doorway looking in at her.*

PETER. See. That's what he needs.

Tentatively, JUNE *strokes the* INDIAN BOY*'s hair.*

You know it is, don't you? Instinct. Can't dismiss instinct
just because you can't grab it out the air like a butterfly and
staple it on a bit of A4.

JUNE. No.

PETER. Don't let him put you off, darlin', looks to me like you know what you're doing.

JUNE studies him for a second, working out if he means it. She laughs.

JUNE. You think so?

PETER. Well, that's my instinct, what do I know, you're the doctor, aren't you?

JUNE. Not yet . . .

PETER. You know what I mean.

I know those woods.

I know what he needs.

JUNE. What?

PETER. He needs to forget them. He needs to be part of the world. Can't go looking for your mum under a bramble bush, can you?

JUNE. Julius and I used to go into those woods.

PETER. Loved-up teenagers. On every woodland path like speed bumps. Nothing changes.

You've got a daughter about that age, haven't you?

JUNE (*surprised*). Yes.

PETER. He thinks the world of the two of you, Julius, you know, whatever madness has got hold of him at the minute.

JUNE. He's not the mad one, that's the problem.

PETER. Oh they all say that.

JUNE laughs again.

He said to me, 'She's like a network of roots, holding me up.'

JUNE. He said that?

PETER. I know. Face like this I can't believe anyone confides in me either. It was when we were looking at the shell of his new house. They look bigger before you put the floors in, empty. Brought it home to him I suppose, what he'd be losing. Family.

Pause. JUNE *is very thoughtful.* PETER *moves to the* INDIAN BOY.

I just want him fixed.

See, I know what it's like.

JUNE. Being lost?

PETER. Oh, I don't know. He's just got to me, is all.

JUNE *is looking at him, suddenly she catches her breath and turns away.*

What is it? What's the matter?

(*Realisation dawning.*) You just saw something, didn't you? What?

JUNE. Nothing.

PETER. What?

JUNE. I saw you being eaten by leaves!

PETER *freezes. For a moment he doesn't move or speak.*

Well, you asked. I am barking, you know. Don't worry about it.

PETER (*shaken*). Well . . . that was . . . unexpected.

JUNE. I've lived in rooms like this one, Mr Fellowes. More than once.

PETER (*still shaky*). Peter. Call me Peter.

JUNE. I'm mad, Peter. I'm just what they call high functioning. I see things that aren't there.

PETER. No. I believe in you.

I've got a . . . phobia . . . whatever . . . I don't like woods. Too . . . empty. Truth is, I'm sure there's something nastier than a teddy bears' picnic waiting in there. I don't like going under the leaves. I can't breathe there.

JUNE. Really?

PETER. Really. You're not mad.

So . . . the clock is ticking. How do we move forward?

JUNE. You're a very strange man. If you don't mind me saying.

PETER (*smiling to take the sting off it*). Well, you'd know.

JUNE. Yeah.

PETER (*rallying*). See, what I'm thinking . . . get your daughter in here. Same age. Can't hurt, can it?

JUNE strokes the INDIAN BOY's hair.

JUNE. That's not exactly a scientific approach.

PETER. Might stir something up though, mightn't it?

JUNE says nothing.

You think I'm mad now, don't you?

JUNE (*thoughtfully*). No. Sara's his age. She might see something all the rest of us have forgotten.

PETER. You'll think about it?

JUNE. I'll think about it.

PETER. And I think you should trust your feelings. I think you should believe what you see.

JUNE. Peter, don't. Truth is, some days I'm on a cocktail of drugs just to touch the edge of 'normal'. I'm so sorry I upset you, I didn't mean to . . .

PETER (*cutting her off*). Never mind that, just tell me, honestly, what you feel when you look at the boy?

Pause.

JUNE. I know I can help him.

PETER. Now we're moving forward again! Time might be nipping at our heels but we can kick its teeth in, can't we?

(*Shaking her hand, beaming.*) Lovely to meet you, Mrs James. Hope I'll see you again. Lovely to see the boy so happy.

He exits.

JUNE strokes the INDIAN BOY's head. He mutters nonsense words again.

JUNE. Are you happy, sweetheart?

INDIAN BOY's *room. A few weeks later.*

JUNE *sits as she was as* SARA *enters and walks slowly into the* INDIAN BOY's *room.*

SARA *watches for a moment, unsettled and vaguely jealous.*

SARA. I'm not supposed to be here, am I?

JUNE. They're all in the staff kitchen eating birthday cake and drinking pomagne.

They're not supposed to be doing that on shift. This place is getting unreal.

SARA. Yes, but I'm not supposed . . .

JUNE (*patting the floor beside herself*). Come here. Sit down a minute.

SARA *obeys reluctantly. She watches her mother stroking the* INDIAN BOY's *hair.*

SARA. Are you supposed to be touching him?

JUNE. It's not a zoo, you know. There aren't rules about feeding the animals.

Why, does it bother you?

SARA. That's a Dad question.

JUNE. Oh, bloody hell . . . you're right. (*Laughing.*) I'm getting too good at this, aren't I?

SARA. Don't laugh at him.

JUNE *says nothing. Just looks at her.*

And don't look at me like that.

JUNE *looks away, still saying nothing.* SARA *sighs heavily.* JUNE *is tense. The* INDIAN BOY *pulls his head out of her lap, he stays close to her for a moment, not looking at her, then he moves quickly away.*

JUNE. Now I've scared him.

SARA. You didn't do anything.

JUNE (*quietly, sadly*). You don't know what I was thinking.

SARA. Well, neither does he.

JUNE sits, disconsolate. SARA sighs impatiently.

Don't go all . . .

JUNE. What?

SARA. It's fine! Everything's fine!

JUNE just looks at her, sad. SARA sighs again and gets up.

JUNE (*stopping her*). You try!

SARA. Try what?

JUNE. Talking to him. (*As SARA hesitates.*) I think I'm too . . .
emotional. He's very sensitive.

SARA. I thought you said he didn't know anything?

JUNE. Not words.

Just sit close to him and wait. See what happens.

*SARA hesitates again, then she sits down between her
mother and the INDIAN BOY.*

The INDIAN BOY moves further away from both of them.

SARA. See, I can't do it either. Why am I here?

JUNE. I want to know what you think . . . about him.

SARA. Why?

JUNE. He's about your age . . .

SARA laughs in disbelief.

I do, really, want to know what you feel about him.

Pause.

SARA. Don't you have to go and see Dad?

JUNE. Yes. (*Still hesitates.*) We're getting on much better.

SARA. Good.

JUNE. We're going to be friends. I promise.

SARA. Good.

Because this is like . . .

JUNE. What?

SARA (*quietly*). Watching the sky tearing off.

Pause. JUNE doesn't move. SARA looks round at her.

JUNE. I can't just leave you here.

SARA. Why not? Isn't he safe?

JUNE looks at the INDIAN BOY.

JUNE. I'll only be five minutes.

SARA. There you go. (*As JUNE still hesitates.*) I've got the key card. I'll be fine, I won't touch anything. If anyone asks I'm waiting for you.

JUNE. All right.

JUNE leaves. SARA breathes out noisily. She sits on the floor. She starts to text on her mobile. Sends it.

A pause, she looks at the INDIAN BOY. He's apparently unaware of her, watching the tree.

A ring tone. The reply text. The INDIAN BOY turns his head, looking at her.

SARA reads the reply and laughs. She looks up and finds the INDIAN BOY watching her.

They stare at each other for a moment, then the INDIAN BOY whistles the same notes as her ring tone. SARA whistles them back. The INDIAN BOY whistles again and adds some more trilling notes. SARA laughs and tries to mimic him. She can't.

After a moment the INDIAN BOY turns his attention back to the treetops. SARA just sits.

After a few moments she starts to cry quietly. The INDIAN BOY turns and looks at her again. SARA doesn't notice. She gets herself under control, mops her face.

The INDIAN BOY looks back at the tree. SARA looks up at him, then she looks up at the tree. They sit in identical positions, just watching the wind in the leaves.

The sound of wind surging through the leaves. At the same time SARA grabs her head and yells in frustration.

At the same time the INDIAN BOY *howls back at the wind.*

SARA *shuts up at once, startled. The* INDIAN BOY *doesn't look at her. He raises his arms to the branches.*

SARA *looks up at the tree.*

SARA (*quietly*). I like your tree.

The INDIAN BOY *makes no sign he's heard her. They sit. The wind surges again. The sound of rain, getting heavier.*

(*A long sigh of relief.*) Rain. I like the rain.

Pause.

The hawthorn branch is still on the floor. The INDIAN BOY *looks at* SARA *directly. He picks up the branch. He puts it in her lap.*

(*Startled.*) Oh!

SARA *looks at him but he gives no further sign he's aware of her.*

Hullo?

Hullo, will you talk to me? Do you want to talk to me?

Nothing.

SARA *looks at the branch. She smells the blossom.*

Thank you.

The sound of the rain gets louder. SARA *sits, waiting, watching the* INDIAN BOY.

Julius's office.

JUNE *is waiting as* JULIUS *looks over her research notes.*

JUNE. How is your lovely new house?

JULIUS. Oh . . . I'm still stuck in the flat. Building work's running late on the whole development apparently. Some bother with . . . tree roots in the foundations . . . or something. (*Reading.*) This is very good. (*Shows her the page he means.*) Very good.

JUNE. Julius, were you upset that I didn't ask you to mentor my PhD?

JULIUS (*laughs*). Hardly.

That wouldn't have been appropriate, would it?

JUNE. No. Of course not. But I wondered if it upset you?

JULIUS (*at a loss*). But . . . That was never going to happen.

JUNE. No.

He looks at her for a moment, puzzled, trying to work out what she's getting at, then he looks back at her notes.

I think I've got used to you not being there. (*As* JULIUS *looks at her inquiringly.*) Since you've moved out. I think I've finally realised you've really gone.

So, of course, I've started to miss you too.

Or maybe it's coming here. (*As he still doesn't speak.*) Maybe it's the weather.

Did I tell you my theory about that? I think the weather might change my mood, I mean really change it. I kept track of all my recent manic episodes and they coincided with really nasty weather, rain, wind, hail. I suggested to Rob that I was actually just a human barometer. He shouldn't give me antidepressants, he should send me off to Madeira for a few sunny months.

JULIUS. Have you been having manic episodes?

JUNE. Oh . . . Just the cleaning, you know.

JULIUS. I loved the cleaning.

JUNE. Oh, didn't you? Oven, fridge and the tops of all the cupboards every day. It was like being married to a housewife, wasn't it?

JULIUS. Like a cheetah with rubber gloves on.

JUNE. Do you remember that time in the woods?

JULIUS. Which . . . ? (*He remembers.*) Oh.

JUNE. Yes. That time. You remember.

I saw him.

JULIUS. Who?

JUNE. That boy. That's what I saw.

A pause. He really doesn't like this. This really saddens him.

(Quietly.) All right.

That's what I believe.

JULIUS. Yes.

JUNE. It seems important. That I tell you.

JULIUS. Yes.

All right. What combo has Rob got you on now, are you still taking . . . ?

JUNE *(interrupting)*. No, no, I meant important for us.

JULIUS *(gently)*. Why?

JUNE *(small)*. Because . . . until the last bit . . . That was a very, very special day for us.

JULIUS. Yes.

JUNE. Julius . . . did you marry me out of pity?

JULIUS *(gently)*. June. I can't do this again . . .

JUNE *(interrupting)*. Because I always think about the moment you popped the question. I'm flat out on a hospital trolley . . .

JULIUS *(under this)*. Yes.

JUNE *(driving over him)*. . . . and they've just swilled a chemist's shop out my stomach, I've got bile and charcoal coming out my nose . . .

JULIUS *(cutting)*. And I thought you looked wonderful. Yes. I can't keep saying this . . .

JUNE *(interrupting)*. Tell me one more time. Please.

JULIUS. That's when I knew you were what I wanted.

JUNE. No one is ever going to call that a healthy impulse, Jules. Are they?

JULIUS *sighs.*

You wanted to mend me . . .

JULIUS. No!

JUNE. What then?! Why do you want this?!

JULIUS. I don't any more, June. I can't.

JUNE. Yes you do. (*As* JULIUS *says nothing.*) You said I was
like a network of roots that held you up.

JULIUS. When?

JUNE. I don't know. You said it to that little house-builder
friend of yours.

JULIUS. He's not a friend.

I didn't say that to him.

JUNE. So it's not true.

JULIUS. It is true.

Pause.

JUNE. I know . . . I do understand why we have to split up.
You're right. We did agree.

I do understand why you're buying a place big enough for
Sara too.

JULIUS (*trying to interrupt*). June . . .

JUNE. No. You're right. She has to have a safe place to go if
I . . . If things are bad again. I know nothing I feel is ever . . .
reliable, but I still feel . . .

She can't go on.

JULIUS. I know.

JUNE. I still want to be with you.

JULIUS. Yes.

*They look at each other. They slowly move together. They
kiss. They start to make love.*

Wood / building site.

At the same time, we see PETER *by the tree on the building site. He has a gun. He fires into the tree. He laughs in delight.*

PETER. Gotcha!

> BRICKS, CHIPPY *and* SPARKS *are looking on.*

BRICKS. What you doing, boss?

PETER. Shooting magpies.

SPARKS. Is that allowed?

PETER. Not if the RSPB see you.

> *He aims at another bird. A clatter of wings, it's evaded him.*

> Yeah, you fly away. I'll get you next time.

> *He looks at them, watching him.*

> What?

BRICKS. Just . . . Never seen you like this, boss.

PETER. Like what?

SPARKS. Didn't have you down as the hunting, shooting, fishing type.

PETER. We are selling a countryside idyll, right?

BRICKS. If you say so.

PETER. Idyll, it's in the brochure, Bricks. Our target market, well-heeled country lovers. Ramblers, real ale freaks with aspirations to trade in their Audis for muddy Land Rovers. This is what they want. They just don't know it.

SPARKS. They want you to shoot magpies?

PETER. Yes.

> All right, example. Last year a little offshore financier bought a lovely little thatched nicety from me. Her country dream. Then she saw the men coming by to shoot the magpies. Oh what a fuss, tears and screaming. She chased them off, she wrote letters to the papers. She won. She kept them out of her cottage garden with its honeysuckle and

apple blossom. And all the little birds sat in her apple trees
and made their nests, tender nests, lined with the feathers of
their own breasts. And she was happy . . . Until half a
hundredweight of magpies dropped off her thatch and ate
every last cheeping chick.

Solution! (*Waves gun.*) Shoot the black and white buggers
before the weekend owners get here.

SPARKS. Right.

PETER. Course the joke is, what does every punter who buys
the rural dream want to complete the picture? (*Waits, they
don't answer.*) A cat! Hilarious, isn't it? A cat! (*Aiming
along the gun barrel, looking for another target.*) Oh, I'd
like to see their faces when puss brings in its first half-eaten
hedge sparrow.

They buy bird seed as well. Have you seen it? In the shop?
One pound fifty-nine for a bag of bird seed!

Still . . . suppose it saves them a few cans of Whiskas.

BRICKS. Boss? Don't you want me to do that?

SPARKS. You'll mess up your suit.

PETER (*still sighting along the gun*). I'm in a good mood,
boys, a very good mood. I feel like being hands-on today.
We'll get these last few trees felled and be done in five
months.

CHIPPY. It's protected timber. Four hundred year old oak. You
need special permission to fell that.

PETER (*still looking for targets*). Says who?

CHIPPY. It's the law.

PETER. Chippy, these are my woods now and I don't need
permission for anything here. You might have a problem
with that but I have your pay cheque.

All your boys are working like billy-oh today, aren't they?
You three feel like joining in?

CHIPPY. I never thought you'd shoot a magpie.

PETER. Oh really? Why not?

CHIPPY. You and magpies.

PETER. What?

CHIPPY. Thought you'd have an understanding.

PETER. I've got a gun in my hands, Chippy.

CHIPPY and SPARKS leave. BRICKS still stands.

BRICKS. Boss?

PETER. You still here?

BRICKS. Need the afternoon off, boss.

That gets PETER's attention.

It's eh . . . Susan . . . The wife she, eh . . . She's moving into her sister's.

PETER. Well, she can pack her own boxes, can't she?

BRICKS. Thought I'd . . . I don't know. Talk to her or, drive them over there. One or the other. You know.

PETER (*kinder*). She won't go, Bricks.

BRICKS. I think she will.

PETER. She won't go. Got a feeling about it. My feelings are never wrong.

Relax. She won't go. It's a beautiful day. Summer's on the way. The sun is shining. The concrete is rising and everyone's in love.

PETER looks round the site in satisfaction.

My land. My house. My place. Mine now. I can feel it. And it is good.

PETER shoulders the gun and exits.

A rustle of leaves, leaves tossing in the wind, light broken and dappled by tossing treetops.

Julius's office, hospital.

At the same time we see JULIUS*'s office.* JUNE *and* JULIUS *are in a sea of leaves. They are still holding each other.* JUNE *looks at the leaves all round her in wonder.*

JUNE. What is it?

JULIUS (*he can't see it*). Nothing. There's no one here. Look at me, this time just look at me, it's all right. I promise.

INDIAN BOY*'s room, hospital.*

At the same time we see SARA *and the* INDIAN BOY, *enveloped in the same storm of leaves.* SARA *jumps up looking round in wonder.*

SARA. What is it?

The INDIAN BOY *is looking straight at her.*

He raises his arms to the leaves and roars the same whispering rushing noise. He starts to move, rushing round the room, moving at her, moving away, roaring like the wind, leaping.

SARA *backs off.*

(*Scared.*) Don't . . .

The INDIAN BOY *goes on moving, faster.*

Stop it!

She runs for the door, fumbles to get out. She escapes and runs.

The INDIAN BOY *is moving, leaping, dancing in the tossing leaves.*

End of Act One.

ACT TWO

Wood / building site. Summer again.

BRICKS, CHIPPY *and* SPARKS, *walk on to the site. It's early morning.*

PETER *is waiting for them, livid.*

PETER. Where is everyone?

BRICKS (*taking in deserted site*). Oh . . . Farting tombsticks.

CHIPPY. It started again yesterday.

PETER. What started!?

SPARKS. It's because of what happened to Steve, isn't it?

BRICKS (*on mobile but talking to* PETER). I'll fix it, boss, I . . . (*His mobile connects.*) Jez? Pick up, pick up, pick up, I am not having this again. You were on a warning last year and the red card is still in your face, so get down here now! Understand? Jez I . . . (*Looks at phone in disbelief.*) Phone's cut out. Give me your phone, Sparks.

SPARKS *looks at his phone.*

SPARKS. No signal.

CHIPPY *is already checking his.*

CHIPPY. Too much electricity in the air, maybe.

PETER. What started?

CHIPPY. It's too quiet.

BRICKS. Of course it's quiet, it's quiet because the thirty-odd men who should be out there putting up walls and digging . . .

CHIPPY (*interrupting*). I mean there's no birds.

They all listen. It is eerily quiet.

BRICKS. Well, thanks, Chippy, yeah, I can appreciate that is the most disconcerting thing about this situation. Forget about the missing plasterers, where are the wood pigeons!?

PETER. What started?

SPARKS. Everything! I wouldn't have come. (*To* BRICKS.)
I wouldn't have come if you hadn't picked me up. Did you
see Steve's leg, did you see it?

BRICKS. Steve was careless. Steve was an idiot. Steve was
asking for ten stitches in his thigh.

SPARKS. The saw just bounced off the tree, just bounced off
the tree as soon as he touched it.

BRICKS. Sorry, boss, he's a bit . . .

SPARKS (*interrupting*). And there's a hornets' nest in the
portaloo . . .

CHIPPY. There's a hornets' nest in every portaloo.

BRICKS. I know! So piss in a ditch!

SPARKS (*to* PETER). I put the wiring in that house yesterday
morning, tested it. Nothing. So I lifted the boards, there's
already green roots all through . . .

BRICKS (*interrupting*). So go and sort it, Sparks!

SPARKS. Green roots had grown all through my wires in half
an hour. They're growing so fast you can see them move!

CHIPPY. Listen!

BRICKS. Oh, what now?

*First one bird alone and then every bird at once. The dawn
chorus.*

CHIPPY. It's the dawn chorus.

BRICKS. Dawn was three hours ago.

CHIPPY. They've must have been waiting for something.
Something as big as a sunrise . . .

PETER (*cutting over him*). Stop right there!

Stop right there or I'll shut you up for good!

PETER *exits. Pause.*

BRICKS (*waving phone.*) I'm going out from under this tree.
You two wait here. (*To* CHIPPY, *indicating* SPARKS.)

Look after him. All right? Calm him down. Give him a cup of tea.

BRICKS *exits or moves further away from the others.*

CHIPPY. Don't have a flask, Sparks.

SPARKS. I don't want a cup of tea. I want to go home.

CHIPPY. Wait a minute, listen to those birds.

SPARKS. I think I'm going to push off home, Chippy.

CHIPPY. Sit down a minute, listen.

Reluctantly SPARKS *does so.*

My father died last year.

He loved birds. I never took much interest. I took it for granted that my dad could point at any feathered thing and give it a name.

At the end he'd started to fret about a lot of things, he worried about what he might be forgetting till he'd barely time to remember anything. He worried about the birds. He said they were disappearing. He worried about losing his glasses, too. They were always disappearing on him. I didn't pay much attention.

When he died I was sorry I hadn't asked him the names of more birds, hadn't learnt, hadn't remembered something that gave him so much pleasure. Dad didn't want a headstone. I took up birdwatching instead. I thought that would be a memorial he would have liked.

But the birds were gone. All the names I remembered, his friends, the little favourites that made his face light up, chiff chaff, mistle thrush, 'little bit of bread and no cheese' yellow hammer. And where are the starlings? Where are they? The telephone wires used to be thick with them. Bandit birds, my dad called them, wheezing and clicking and wolf whistling over every dawn chorus. Gone. All gone. It made me so angry. It made me so unhappy. I wanted to do this to remember my dad and every bird I looked for, I had to mourn him all over again.

SPARKS *is only half-listening, looking nervously round the site, craning to see after* BRICKS.

CHIPPY *watches the birds for a moment. He smiles.*

Still got a few, though. Look at him.

SPARKS (*wheeling*). Where?

CHIPPY. There, see him all red and gold? Goldfinch. Red face, I call him.

SPARKS. Red face?

CHIPPY. Look, see? Bright red above his bill. He's rare these days. He has these little hard red feathers all over his face, like a red lacquer mask, he can push his face right into a thistle and never feel it, eat the seeds. He's got the sweetest song. That's been the death of him, his song.

They trapped him, for hundreds of years, thousands of finches caught and kept in cages for their song. They still do that over in Europe. Don't know what they do if they don't sing . . . I expect they kill them then, or let them go. They eat little birds over there. We haven't got enough of them left to eat.

Blackbirds in a pie. Might still manage that one.

SPARKS. Chippy, I'm really not happy being here.

CHIPPY. Me neither but I've still ten grand of debts. (*Hearing another bird.*) That's another I know! I'm getting lucky today. That's a chaffinch. That's his rain song. If you hear that, get your brolly out, the rain's coming.

He looks up at the sky.

SPARKS. It's starting again, isn't it? Worse.

CHIPPY. Bigger. (*Listening.*) He's warning us, rain and storm coming. Listen.

Lazy little sod.

SPARKS. Who?

CHIPPY. The chaffinch. Male bird does nothing. He sits there whistling and the hen builds the whole nest. He never so much as picks up a twig. She does it all.

But she's only got one tree to build a nest in now, hasn't she?

Peter Fellowes is an evil little shit.

He said they wouldn't fell all the trees. He said the boy'd be looked after. We shouldn't have let him take the boy, Sparks. Do you think it was a real boy?

SPARKS. Oh, don't start on that again, Chippy, my nerves are unravelled . . .

CHIPPY. Maybe he really was someone's disposable kid, return to sender, faulty merchandise. Or maybe I saw what my granny saw, an elfin prince still living in the greenwood. And maybe we walked away while Peter Fellowes and Bricks tore that last bit of magic out of the woods for ever.

SPARKS. I can't listen to this, Chippy . . .

CHIPPY. No, I've had to take to the whisky again. Once you've let words like elf or fairy out your mouth there's no other option. It's that or join the Brownies.

The thing is. If it's real . . . it's not for kids, is it? If it's real. It's not safe at all.

I know what needs to be stopped. He needs to be stopped.

CHIPPY *walks off.*

SPARKS. Well, don't leave me!

He hurries after him, colliding with BRICKS, *who is entering, carrying a chainsaw.*

BRICKS. Where are you off to? Walked right back to the van. Not even one bar. You better help me with this.

SPARKS. With what?

BRICKS. Taking this last tree out.

The hospital. INDIAN BOY*'s room / corridor.*

Inside the INDIAN BOY*'s room, the* INDIAN BOY *is watching the tree, swaying, dancing.*

Outside in the corridor JUNE *and the* NURSE *are bathed in sunlight, breathing in the air from open windows above them.*

The NURSE *is sitting on the floor, eating a honeycomb out of a jar with her fingers. She is now nearly nine months pregnant.*

The sound of singing, a man's voice, amateur, shaky but passionate, singing a fifties love ballad.

There are wild flowers scattered on the floor. JUNE *is half-singing to the music, dancing along. Every so often she picks up another flower from the floor.*

NURSE. Do you know how much this stuff costs?

JUNE. A lot?

NURSE. Oh . . . it'd be cheaper to learn how to keep bees.

I had to have the comb you see. Something about . . . biting through the wax . . . *(Does so.)* Oh! *(Ecstasy.)* Oh, that's too good. Oh, that'll knock me out. Oh, thank the angels for cravings . . . mmmmmmm! *(Licks her fingers.)* You can taste the flowers.

JUNE *(picking one up)*. Where did these flowers come from?

NURSE. I don't know.

I think one of the day-release patients brought them in. Which would be a miracle, because the only one who's back today is Beryl, and she hasn't smiled since nineteen ninety-five, and that was when the orderly skidded on a little incontinence event and knocked herself out on the door frame.

Beryl wouldn't smell a rose if you starved her for a week and then offered her one dipped in chocolate.

There's a daisy chain all the way up the stairs, wound in and out of the bannisters.

Of course, one of the minimum security patients could have climbed out these windows and out onto the lawn . . .

JUNE. We all needed fresh air though, didn't we?

NURSE. That's exactly what I thought. Fresh air and sunlight. You can't beat the old-fashioned remedies.

JUNE. Where are all the other staff?

NURSE. Sunbathing. It's a lovely day.

JUNE. Who's singing?

NURSE. Earl.

> Which is a surprise because he was long-term catatonic. He
> hasn't moved. His eyes are still shut. But he's lying there,
> singing his lungs out . . .

JUNE. What does Julius think of it all?

NURSE. You tell me.

> You know I can't see it actually.

JUNE. What?

NURSE. You and Dr James. No offence.

JUNE. Nineteen years, on and off.

NURSE. No!

JUNE. Somehow we always came back together. Because
together we still made sense.

NURSE. What did you make apart?

JUNE. Misery.

> I'm mad and he isn't, that's how it works.

NURSE. Who says you're mad? Him?

JUNE (*smiling*). Oh, that's one of the few things we agree
about.

NURSE. Well, I've worked here twelve years and I'm telling
you, 'mad' doesn't mean anything.

JUNE. That's what Julius says too. (*Picking up flowers again,
quiet, happy.*) We were students together, then I was in a
place like this one . . . then he was my supervisor . . . then
I was in another place like this one . . . then we got married
and I'm someone else's patient now. Someone else's
student. (*Looking round.*) You know what, I'm lying, I was
never in a place like this one. You lot are crap on security.

NURSE. You think?

JUNE. I'm not complaining, just every time I come . . .

NURSE. It's been a strange few months, now I think about it.

> It's just getting more relaxed though, isn't it?

JUNE. Have you ever worked on a ward like this one? Look around. It's not relaxed. It's unbelievable!

NURSE. But it's nice. Even Mowgli's so much happier.

JUNE (*dancing again*). Oh, I'm not complaining. I don't come here to work any more. I come here for the dancing.

NURSE. Do you think Dr James'll be upset . . . about the windows?

JUNE stops dancing, she looks up at the windows, considering.

JUNE. No. Why should he be?

NURSE. That's what I thought. It's not as if its raining, is it? (*She offers JUNE some honey.*) Want some?

JUNE shakes her head. She hums, picking up more flowers.

The NURSE eats more honey. The song changes, something more up-tempo. JUNE looks at the NURSE, she holds out her hands.

JUNE. Come on.

The NURSE hesitates then gets up, laughing, still holding her honey jar. They dance together, twirling and giggling, dancing off. JUNE's workbag lies abandoned on the floor.

INDIAN BOY (*moving with the tree*). Red face, red face . . .

Kill me or let me go. I won't sing.

Light split my head open. He can do it. Split me open. Kill me or let me go. I won't sing.

Under this, SARA edges on. She looks in her mother's bag. She gets out her security card. She opens the INDIAN BOY's door. He is instantly silent.

She watches him for a moment. He doesn't react to her presence at all, still looking at the tree. SARA hesitates then moves close him, watching him intently.

She touches him. He suffers the touch but doesn't acknowledge it.

SARA. I was afraid to come back before. I'm sorry.

Nothing.

I told Mum I never wanted to come back. I cried. I was really scared.

But I've dreamt about you every night.

I don't know why.

I had to see you.

I don't know why.

Still nothing.

(*Moving closer.*) Your hair is like fur under my hands. And when I touch it, when I touch you, I feel like I'm stroking a huge cat, big enough to lie on top of me. Powerful enough to break my ribs. I want you to lick me with a tiger's tongue, I want to hold your fur. I would follow you anywhere.

The INDIAN BOY *turns his head and looks at her.* SARA *is upset.*

You weren't supposed to understand.

I didn't think you could understand.

He doesn't move or change expression. After a moment she looks in her bag. She takes out a rose in plastic wrapping. She offers it then puts it down next to him. He stops moving and looks at it.

He bends his head and sniffs it without touching it. SARA *takes it back.*

Here.

She pulls off the plastic wrapping and puts the rose back beside him.

Gingerly he picks it up. He sniffs it. He licks it. He bites into the flower.

Hey!

The INDIAN BOY *lets the remains of the rose fall and watches the tree, chewing now.*

He looks at her again, then he moves over he sniffs her delicately, then he runs his tongue up the side of her neck.

He looks in her face.

He lays his head in her lap.

After a moment SARA *reaches out and starts to stroke his head.*

JULIUS*'s office.*

JULIUS *comes in.* PETER *is already sitting in his chair.*

JULIUS. What are you doing . . . ?

PETER (*interrupting*). There were charcoal burners living in those woods until the wolves drove them out. Poor charcoal burner lost his little limping toddler to a hungry she-wolf. Imagine how he felt, eh? Hunted to extinction? Yeah well, look at it from the charcoal burners point of view, they were asking for it, weren't they?

Any father's going to get angry if someone makes his daughter into dog meat, isn't he!? Come and look at the boy with me, Julius. I think its time to get angry.

JULIUS *approaches carefully. He gets himself on the same eye level as* PETER.

JULIUS. Peter . . . I don't think you should visit Ajay any more.

I think it upsets you.

Pause.

PETER. I'm not upset.

JULIUS. I think you are.

PETER. Well, you don't know me, do you?

JULIUS. You were abandoned in those woods.

Weren't you?

Pause.

PETER. That was a long time ago.

What about it?

JULIUS. I'm not the person you should talk to about it anyway, I'm not that kind of . . .

PETER. I don't want to talk to anyone. What's the point in talking?

JULIUS. It might help.

PETER. Oh, you think?

JULIUS. If you want help.

PETER (*interrupting*). Oh, it ruined my life. Ruined it. And I've had a long life. But what about it? Time rolls on, doesn't it, and here we are skipping ahead of it . . .

JULIUS (*cutting in*). How old were you?

PETER. When?

JULIUS. When your parents left you?

PETER. I've no idea. I don't even understand the question.

JULIUS. About his age.

PETER. Have I annoyed you or something?

JULIUS. You talked to my wife.

PETER. Oh. Now we're getting to it. Yes.

JULIUS. Why?

PETER. Did I need permission? Very old-fashioned attitude, Julius. Do you read her mail as well?

JULIUS. You told her something, something I said . . . I didn't say it. You made it up.

PETER. But was it true?

JULIUS *says nothing.*

And how have you two been getting on since?

JULIUS. Why are you involving yourself?

PETER. I'm just taking an interest. I'm just taking an interest because you're taking care of the boy, but there's things you don't know about that boy . . .

JULIUS. You said you didn't know him. You said you'd never seen him before.

PETER. I know those woods.

I know . . .

He stops.

JULIUS. What?

PETER. Why is there moss growing on your skirting boards?

JULIUS (*looking*). We're having problems . . . with the air conditioning . . . humidity levels.

PETER. Oh, humidity levels! I see.

Probably doesn't help that you've got all the windows open.

JULIUS. What windows?

PETER. Every window along the corridor out there.

JULIUS. Those windows don't open.

PETER. Well . . . looks like someone fixed that, didn't they? Which is a shame, because now anything can get in or out, can't it?

JULIUS *gives a sigh of exasperation and snatches up the phone, punching in an extension number.*

Are you paying attention yet, Julius? The boy needs sorting out. I know him. I know.

JULIUS. You said you had never seen the boy before.

PETER. No. But everyone's heard the stories.

JULIUS. What stories?

PETER. Well, I don't believe them either but I think something's up. I think the cunning little pup's got more going on than you can tell by looking at him. I think he's too frisky. I think you should shut his brain down for him. That's my advice.

JULIUS (*exasperated on phone, he's got through to an answering machine*). This is Dr James, would one of the ward staff report to me at once?

PETER. No one there? The whole place is deserted, as far as I can make out.

JULIUS. What are you talking about? Shut his brain down for him?

PETER. You know the old, eh . . . (*Mimes whacking someone.*) Chemical cosh.

Pause.

JULIUS. He had head injuries when he came in.

PETER *says nothing.*

You hit him, didn't you?

PETER. I never touched him.

JULIUS. You know him.

PETER. I know his type.

JULIUS. What type is that?

PETER. I know better than you.

JULIUS. A boy, abandoned in the woods . . .

PETER. You haven't a clue what you are dealing with.

JULIUS. So tell me what I'm dealing with.

PETER. All right, don't believe me. 'Go and see for yourself. Go on. Go and look at the treacherous little wasp.'

I tried. I tried, Julius, I don't understand it.

We're all in trouble now. Do it your way, it's up to you now.

Look at what he's doing and if you can stop it then believe me, you have to, whatever it takes.

PETER *goes to leave, he stops.*

The sky is falling down. I'm serious. Don't ask me how I know. I just know!

He's trouble. He's trouble. I'll do what I can my end but you've got to help. You've got to stop this.

PETER *leaves. The sky darkens. The first, distant, rumble of thunder.*

JULIUS *moves out of his office. He sees the open windows, scattered flowers.*

*He fights to close the high windows as the sky grows darker
and rain starts to pelt down.*

He closes the first window with a bang.

The INDIAN BOY *starts up out of* SARA*'s lap and flattens
himself against the wall, hissing in alarm.*

The second window closes with a bang.

SARA. It's all right, come back, it's all right.

The third window bangs shut.

The INDIAN BOY *drops and covers his head with his
hands.* SARA *crosses to him, trying to stroke him. He's
completely unresponsive.*

JULIUS *comes into the room.*

JULIUS. What are you doing, Sara? How did you find your
way in here?

SARA (*distressed*). He's scared. Look at him!

JULIUS *doesn't move for a moment.*

Help him!

JULIUS *crosses to her and gently moves her away from the*
INDIAN BOY.

JULIUS. He's safe. Sara. It's all right. He's safe. Calm down.

SARA (*still distressed*). But he's upset.

JULIUS. He's quite safe. Nothing's wrong. It's all right.

SARA *calms.*

What are you doing here?

SARA. I'm not doing anything wrong, am I?

JULIUS. No . . . no, of course not, sweetheart.

Where's your mother?

SARA. I'm waiting for her.

JULIUS (*gently*). You shouldn't be in here.

SARA. She told me she wanted me to watch him. For her
research.

JULIUS. What research?

SARA. She's doing her PhD on him.

Pause.

JULIUS. That's not the research she's been showing me.

SARA. Well . . . that's what she's planning.

JULIUS *slumps.*

JULIUS. Where is she?

SARA. I don't know. She'll be back soon.

JULIUS *(really angry).* She's been lying to me. She's been lying to me! Why is she still doing that?

SARA. I don't know. Sorry. Sorry.

JULIUS. Don't be, you haven't done anything.

SARA. Yes. No. Sorry.

JULIUS. Don't be. Stop saying that!

SARA. Sorry. Oh . . .

SARA *is hunched, tense, echoing the* INDIAN BOY.

JULIUS *backs off.*

JULIUS. No, I'm sorry. I'm sorry.

Pause.

SARA. It was only one time before today . . .

She thought I might know what he wants. She wanted to know how I felt about him.

I think he wants to go outside.

JULIUS. Last time he was outside he broke away from three nurses and ran straight out in front of a bus.

When did you first visit?

SARA. I don't know.

A few weeks ago.

JULIUS. He stopped eating a few weeks ago.

Pause. They look at the INDIAN BOY, *he's moving again.*

SARA (*small*). I just saw him eat.

JULIUS. What did he eat?

SARA. A flower.

JULIUS. All right. To be precise, he stopped eating food with any nutritional value. He has eaten part of a potted fern and a few woodlice.

The diagnostic team were at a loss to pinpoint what had happened, what had changed in his routine.

SARA. The nurse said he was happier.

JULIUS. Would this be Nurse Robertson? The one who calls him Mowgli?

Pause.

SARA. I don't know.

JULIUS. Well, we'll find out.

SARA. I didn't know. I'm sorry.

JULIUS. Please stop saying that.

He crosses to the INDIAN BOY. *He checks him over, basic medical checks, gentle.* SARA *watches.*

How are things at home at the moment?

SARA. Fine.

JULIUS. The school report was very good. I'm very proud of you.

SARA. Thanks.

JULIUS. You know you can always ring if you need me. You can always count on my support. Don't feel you're alone with this.

SARA. With what?

JULIUS. Is she still keeping her weekly appointment with Rob? Dr Taylor?

SARA. I don't know.

JULIUS. He says she's skipped the last few sessions.

SARA. Well, I don't know what she's doing.

She's been happy.

JULIUS. Has she?

SARA. Yes. It's been nice.

JULIUS. Come on. I'll walk you out.

He ushers her out into the corridor and locks the door behind them.

Sara. Would it be easier for you if you came and lived with me for a while?

SARA (*in a small voice*). Aren't you coming home this time, after all?

JULIUS. What did your mother say?

SARA. She said . . .

(*Upset*). She said everything was better. She said it was all fixed again.

JULIUS *sighs.*

A rumble of thunder. The INDIAN BOY *stirs.*

JULIUS. Sara, just tell me what you want. It's all right. Do you want to come with me? Don't be scared. Just tell me what you really want to do.

SARA (*quietly*). It doesn't make any difference what I want. Just tell me what's going to happen.

Another rumble. The INDIAN BOY *is up. He flattens himself against the door.*

JULIUS (*starting to move off*). We'll talk about it.

The INDIAN BOY *is bumping against the door, banging against it, gentle at first.*

INDIAN BOY. She'll leave the eggs in the nest, inside cold and curled and soft for ever, cold for ever, feather and bone . . .

SARA has stopped, hearing the movement against the door.

SARA. He's moving. He's still upset.

JULIUS. What?

INDIAN BOY. Sharp ears will find his own small ones. Blind and pink and milk wet. He smells her on them and he eats them all, eats them all, wriggling in his throat, and then the sky is touching the earth and tearing it up . . .

SARA. He wants to get out.

JULIUS *has moved back to the door.*

JULIUS. He's a little agitated, that's all. He'll calm down in a moment.

JULIUS *observes the boy. The* INDIAN BOY *is throwing himself against the door now.*

INDIAN BOY. Light splits the sky. Wind like a bear through the trees. Tree fell down all his green crown broken on his head. All fell with him. Black jagged wing flew up and off into storm sky. Powder wing and thousand leg torn away and blown away like dead leaves. Eggs smashed and honey crushed, stripe coat thousands crawling blind and mad. Pin wing bald chicks gaped their mouths and died.

JULIUS. Sara, go back to the car. I have to deal with this.

SARA. I want to stay. He's upset.

INDIAN BOY (*over this*). Black coat, hard coat runs away, runs away, runs away. His home is gone.

JULIUS. Sara, please do what I tell you.

SARA. No! I want to stay with him!

INDIAN BOY (*over this*). Tree gone, home gone, water big enough to drown him, still he runs, looking for tree . . .

JULIUS. Stand over there.

Another rumble of thunder. SARA *backs off reluctantly.*

INDIAN BOY. . . . looking for home, over stone, and twig and swept away by water he runs and runs . . . He never finds tree. He never finds home. Now he's dead.

JULIUS *is about to unlock the* INDIAN BOY*'s door.*

The NURSE *and* JUNE *dance back along the corridor outside the* INDIAN BOY*'s room, still laughing.*

They stop dead when they see JULIUS, *instantly guilty.*

Thunder.

Earth fights sky and we're all dead.

The INDIAN BOY *goes still, pressed against the door.*

JULIUS. Nurse Roberts.

NURSE. Doctor.

JULIUS. Why were these windows open?

NURSE. I'm sorry, Doctor, I didn't know it was going to rain.

JUNE (*interrupting*). Fresh air, Julius!

JULIUS (*ignoring her*). When did I authorise Mrs James to have access to patient Ajay?

JUNE. Sunlight, Julius!

NURSE. You said key card and badge, you didn't say limited access, you didn't say . . . I thought . . .

JUNE (*cutting in*). Ooooh, Julius, now if you're not precise with your language we all know you're unlikely to be precise in your thinking. Very naughty.

(*Reacting to his expression.*) Lighten up, will you!

JULIUS (*turning on her*). Lighten up!?

Where are we, Nurse Roberts?

NURSE. Eh . . . ?

JULIUS. The medium security section of a psychiatric unit. A real one. A real hospital spitting distance from Coventry. Not a movie hospital, not a psychiatric unit in a Hollywood back lot. So I hate to break it to you, June, but the effects of 'sunlight' and 'fresh air' are not going to be as miraculous as you imagine.

If you run through the wards urging the patients to throw off their chemical shackles half of them will require extra sedation for a week.

If you frolic through the security doors with flowers in your hair provoking our more disturbed patients to make a grab for the bluebird of happiness, someone will probably lose an eye.

If it was that simple, Nurse Roberts, human misery could be solved by a charismatic clown making balloon animals.

If it was *that simple*, June, tortured and abused children could be cured by handing them a bunch of buttercups and telling them it wasn't their fault.

(*To* NURSE.) You know better!

(*To* JUNE.) And you! . . . Oh, you know better!

NURSE. It's just . . . it was such a lovely day, Dr James. And the air conditioning isn't working . . .

Another rumble of thunder, then singing pitched over it. Another love ballad.

The INDIAN BOY *is still pressed to the door, listening.* JUNE *has seen* SARA.

JUNE. Sara honey, wait at the car, don't...

SARA *backs off further under this but doesn't leave.*

JULIUS (*cutting in on* JUNE). Why did you lie to me?

JUNE. Julius . . . that day, we walked into the trees . . .

JULIUS. June . . .

JUNE. You saw it too! You said I've never seen light like this . . . and we heard . . .

JULIUS. Jesus, you've stopped taking your prescription, haven't you?

JUNE. *You* heard it! You said is that in my ears or can you hear music and we lay down . . .

JULIUS. All right, that is just . . . We were nineteen! We were high!

JUNE. And afterwards I looked up into the leaves and I saw him! (*Pointing at the* INDIAN BOY's *room.*) It was him, Julius!

And beyond him . . . a whole . . . a whole other . . . it was too much, too much to look at, I came apart, but I believe I saw it, Julius! And so did you!

JULIUS. I saw the leaves.

June, you have to take your prescription *now* . . .

(*Re the singing.*) Where's that coming from?

NURSE. It's Earl, Dr James. He's singing.

JULIUS. But . . . he's catatonic.

NURSE. I know. I know, Dr James, I can't explain it either, something in the air today.

JUNE *holds out her arms as the music continues over the sound of rain and thunder.*

JUNE. Julius, dance with me.

He seems torn. She smiles, stepping towards him.

Just for a moment.

He seems to accept, relaxing into her arms. Then he has a firm hold of her wrist.

Ow! Julius let go!

In his room, the INDIAN BOY *is pacing now, up and down.*

JULIUS. June. I'm sorry. You've just proved you can't be trusted to protect your own best interests.

JUNE. You're *hurting* me!

JULIUS. Sara was in a locked room with a patient! Alone!

JUNE. No, she wasn't! She sits in the waiting room with her homework. She never wanted to go back. It was one time and I . . .

JULIUS (*cutting her off*). You involved our daughter in an abuse of my trust, of our patient's trust . . .

JUNE. Maybe that trust is misplaced! Maybe you're wrong, Julius! Did you think of that?!

JULIUS. Well, I'm always wrong, June! That's my role, isn't it? That was decided a long time ago, wasn't it!? But unfortunately for you, I'm not the one deemed by the courts to be a danger to myself and others, am I?!

SARA *puts her hands over her ears.*

SARA (*quietly*). Stop it. Stop it.

The INDIAN BOY *is moving to and fro, faster, frantic now.*

JULIUS. I'm bringing a petition for custody.

JUNE. She's nearly fifteen. She makes up her own mind.

JULIUS. Not if she's not living in a safe place. She comes with me now!

There is another rumble of thunder.

JUNE. You bastard, Julius!

SARA. Stop it.

Another rumble of thunder. The boom of a lightning strike. The lights go out. JULIUS *and* JUNE *barely notice.*

NURSE. Dr James, the power's gone!

JUNE. You fucking *bastard!*

JULIUS. June. When you lose control . . .

JUNE (*interrupting*). When I lose control you get hard, Julius.

NURSE. The emergency lights haven't come on, Dr James! Something's wrong!

JULIUS *tries to get a stronger hold of* JUNE. *The* INDIAN BOY *is hurling round his room, banging, scrabbling for a way out. There is the sound of running feet. Voices shouting, agitated.*

JUNE (*wrenching away*). Don't touch me!

NURSE. All right both of you! Both of you stop this right now!

JUNE. Stop it! Don't touch me!

She's hits out at JULIUS, *attacking him.*

SARA. Stop it!

NURSE. The door locks, Dr James! The door locks have shorted!

JULIUS *is trying to restrain* JUNE. *She's going crazy now.*

SARA *runs. She runs to the* INDIAN BOY's *door, pressing against it.*

JULIUS *grabs* JUNE *and holds her down. She fights back, kicking and scratching.*

SARA. Stop it!

JUNE starts to scream.

JULIUS (*to* NURSE). Mrs James is an out patient at the hospital. She is a patient of Dr Taylor's. She's distraught and she needs ten ccs of *tranquiliser*, now!

SARA is banging on the INDIAN BOY*'s door.*

SARA. Stop it! I'll let you out. I'll let you go out, please, please stop.

JULIUS. Now, Nurse!

NURSE. I'll stick a needle in your arse first! Stop it! Look around you! The door locks have shorted! Dr James, let her go!

Another rumble of thunder. The INDIAN BOY *goes still, staring at the door.*

The NURSE *is wading in, whacking at both* JULIUS *and* JUNE.

Will the two of you . . . (*Slap.*) Stop messing about like a couple of spoilt babies . . . (*Slap.*) And look at what's going on!

Suddenly she doubles over, clutching herself.

Oh! Oh no!

She's holding her pregnancy, terrified. JUNE *and* JULIUS *have stopped struggling, staring at the* NURSE.

(*Grinning.*) Made you look. (*She winces.*) Oh shit, no, I really am starting!

JUNE and JULIUS *hurry to help her.* SARA *pushes at the door. It opens. She looks in at the* INDIAN BOY *for a shocked moment, then she moves to him.*

SARA (*pulling at* INDIAN BOY). Get up. Come on. Get up. I'll take you outside. All the doors are open. I'll let you see the tree.

Slowly he gets up.

Hold my hand. You have to hold my hand.

He takes her hand.

You musn't run away. You musn't let go my hand. Promise me. Don't let go my hand.

SARA *leads him forward. The exit.*

JULIUS *and* JUNE *are helping the* NURSE *up.* JUNE *leans on* JULIUS *as they do so. He kisses her briefly.*

NURSE (*watching*). Oh, for the love of . . . Listen, if that is what you two do for fun you need to take it down a notch or two. Take up bridge or something, birdwatching . . . join a nice wine club or . . .

(*The pain starts again.*) Ooooh, this isn't going to be fun, is it?

JUNE *looks round.*

JUNE. Sara?

Outside the hospital, in front of the INDIAN BOY*'s tree.*

SARA *and the* INDIAN BOY *are outside. A roar of leaves, lashed with wind and rain.*

SARA. There. Now you can see your tree.

They look up. The INDIAN BOY*'s face is full of wonder.*

It's big, when you look at it, isn't it? Very big, and all of it's moving.

The INDIAN BOY *looks for a moment then he pulls his hand from hers and runs, flat out.*

No! No! Come back! Come back!

The INDIAN BOY *is gone.*

SARA *runs after him.*

Please! Come back!

The tree tossing in a growing storm.

The forest glade at the edge of the building site.

First we just hear the roar of a chainsaw, scream of blade straining against something solid, a bang, a yell of pain.

Then we see BRICKS, *standing at the base of the tree. He has the remains of a chainsaw in his hands. Its teeth are mangled. The motor is smoking.*

BRICKS *has a bleeding hole in his leg. He is looking at it with mild consternation.*

SPARKS *sits some distance away, whimpering and trying to stuff plastic bags in his ears.*

BRICKS *sways.* PETER *comes on and stops dead at the sight of him.*

BRICKS (*to* PETER, *outraged*). Now this is exactly what happened to the Steve, what are the fucking odds!?

> BRICKS *falls over.* PETER *runs to him.* SPARKS *doesn't even notice.*

PETER. You're all right.

BRICKS. I'm not. I've got a hole in my leg the size of Warwick.

PETER. You're going to be fine.

BRICKS. I'm bleeding out like a hosepipe after the lawn mower's been at it.

> PETER *is working fast, getting his tie off, to use as a tourniquet on* BRICKS's *leg.*

PETER (*to* SPARKS). Hey. Hey!

> SPARKS *is still trying to fit the plastic bags in his ears.*

(*To* BRICKS.) What's wrong with him?

BRICKS. He says he can hear music.

I don't know what he's complaining about. Saves buying an iPod, doesn't it?

Half the walls fell down, too. It's the tree roots, boss. They keep growing up through the bricks.

PETER. What tree roots?! We've cut down all the trees!

BRICKS. 'Cept this one.

I had a go, boss. And I was careful.

Fucking saw bounces off it like it's made of granite, straight into my leg. Just like Steve. What are the odds?

PETER. You're a bricklayer. What do you know about chainsaws?

BRICKS. Steve knew about chainsaws. Didn't save him a ride in the ambulance, did it? Have you called the ambulance, boss?

PETER *swears under his breath and pulls out his mobile.*

BRICKS. Don't want to rush you but, you know, feeling a bit light-headed.

PETER (*on phone*). Ambulance please.

BRICKS. Wow, look at that. What network are you on then? It's my anniversary next week. If I go and die before our anniversary it'll break my heart. I've got the restaurant booked and everything.

PETER (*on phone*). Yes, hullo, I'm the building site in Peaswood, Oak Lane. I've got a workman here who's put a chainsaw into his leg. (*Looking at leg.*) About six inches.

BRICKS. Ten centimetres, boss. Can I get the phone when you're done? I keep telling you to get metric.

PETER. All right. Will do. Thanks.

PETER *cuts call and sets about elevating* BRICKS' *leg.*

BRICKS. I tell you something, boss. Something definitely doesn't want us building here. Can I borrow the phone?

PETER (*working*). Oh, you think I'm just going to give up? Back off? Fade away?

BRICKS. The phone, boss?

PETER. What for?

BRICKS (*leg in agony as* PETER *moves it*). Aaaargh! Shit!

Want to phone Susan. Tell her I love her before I die.

PETER. You're not going to die.

BRICKS. But suppose I do?

PETER. You won't!

BRICKS. But suppose I do? You see it in films all the time. He pegs out in a bomb crater or down a crocodiles gullet and never even lets her know he cares. Regrets it for ever.

PETER. Well, you won't regret it for ever will you? You'll be dead.

BRICKS. Aaaargh! That is it! I am going to haunt you so bad you'll have to hire the Pope to get rid of me!

PETER. Here!

Hands BRICKS *the phone.* BRICKS *struggles to punch the numbers.*

Come on, Bricks. I need you back at work. You're strong, your sinews will knit like willow roots.

BRICKS (*his call has connected*). Ooh, here we go. (*Listens.*) Aw, it's the machine.Where's she gone then? (*Into phone.*) Susan? I eh . . . I've had a bit of an accident. They're taking me up the hospital, so, eh . . . I just wanted to say . . . (*Long struggling pause.*) Could you go round our place and bring up my shaving stuff and my tracky bottoms and a tee shirt? Cheers, darlin'. See you later. (*Cuts call. Sees* PETER *looking at him accusingly.*) Feelings like that go deep. Deep inside. That's where they are. Inside. How are you supposed to get them out and wave them round with five minutes notice? It's not natural.

PETER. You'll be fine. I know. I've got a feeling about it.

BRICKS. You said she wouldn't leave.

PETER. What?

BRICKS. You just had a feeling. She wasn't going to leave. I worked the afternoon, got home and found a note on the door and the kiddies' toys all gone. Been living off chips and . . . misery.

She won't come to no restaurant.

I don't believe in your feelings any more, boss.

SPARKS *give a sigh of relief and pulls the plastic out of his ears.*

SPARKS. Oh, thank Christ! Thank Christ it's stopped!

Sees PETER *and* BRICKS. *He's on his feet. Pointing at* PETER.

See!? See!?

We told you it was bad luck! We told you! We're not supposed to be here! Something doesn't want us to build here!

PETER *suddenly explodes; terrifyingly, he snatches up an axe.*

PETER. I am supposed to be here! I want to build here! I'm going to build here!

PETER *looks up at the sky.*

(*Quietly, to himself.*) This is what comes of trying to be kind. What a useless habit that is, eh? Should have known. Well . . . Everything's a bit upside-down now, isn't it? The earth's rising up and the sky is falling down.

CHIPPY *comes on.*

And where have you been!?

CHIPPY. Phoning the police.

PETER. What!?

CHIPPY (*pointing at the tree*). Protected woodland! You can't touch it! It's the law!

PETER *gapes then he starts to laugh.*

PETER. Well, thank our stars for law and order, eh? That'll sort everything. That'll fix it! Everything's all right now!

The INDIAN BOY *runs on and is up the tree in a flash.*

Thunder.

BRICKS. Boss!

SPARKS. Bricks!

CHIPPY. It's all right!

It's all right. He's come home.

PETER *starts to cut down the tree.* CHIPPY *runs forward, grabbing his arm.*

No!

PETER. Get him off me, Bricks.

BRICKS. I can't even stand up!

PETER. Sparks!

SPARKS *is already backing off.*

(*To* CHIPPY.) You're fired. Let go now or you'll be dead.

CHIPPY. You musn't!

PETER *raises the axe. He's strong and* CHIPPY *can't hold his arm. He swings it,* CHIPPY *is knocked flying and falls. He's injured, can't get up.*

PETER *cuts deep into the tree. The* INDIAN BOY *starts to howl, long cries of anguish.* SARA *runs on, putting herself between him and the tree.*

SARA. Stop it!

He stops.

PETER. Come on. Get back.

He waves the axe at her.

BRICKS. Hey! Boss! No . . .

CHIPPY. Leave her!

PETER. I will not hurt you, you stupid little *rabbit*! That tree is unstable! Get back out of it!

Over there!

He points, she moves over by CHIPPY.

SPARKS. You don't pay us for this! You can't . . . .

PETER (*cutting him off*). I will put a rock in your mouth!

SPARKS *subsides.* PETER *turns to* SARA.

What are you doing here?

SARA. I followed him.

PETER *sighs wearily.*

PETER. Oh, for...

Everything is upside down, you see? Everything!

You weren't supposed to follow him! He was supposed to follow you!

Nothing I try works, everything's upside down. My instincts are . . . *bad.* I don't understand . . .

BRICKS. Boss, I don't feel too good.

CHIPPY (*to* SARA). Are you all right?

SARA (*upset*). I couldn't run like he could. I couldn't keep up. I nearly . . . He ran into traffic . . . we nearly died. I couldn't keep up.

BRICKS. Hullo? Anyone listening to the man bleeding to death!?

PETER. I don't have time for this!

PETER *starts chopping again. The* INDIAN BOY *starts howling.* SPARKS *breaks.*

SPARKS. That's it! I'm off!

SPARKS *exits. The* INDIAN BOY *vanishes back into the leaves.*

SARA. He's going to fall!

PETER (*chopping*). I am saving you from madness, you ungrateful mess of maggots!

(*Chops.*) If no one believes in all this, if no one remembers it, it'll have to stop.

(*Chops.*) No one remembers except him. I tried to be gentle, I tried to let nature take its course, but there's no time now. *He's got to be stopped!*

CHIPPY. You've killed these woods! Haven't you done enough!?

PETER (*stops, breathless*). You'd think so, wouldn't you . . .

He looks round the building site.

I was going to be happy in that house. I was going to fit in at last.

A garden. Lots of sunlight.

Time was, you could run from one side of the country to the other and never feel the sun on the back of your neck. Like living under a dark leafy cloud. Only way you could see the sky was to run over the tops of the leaves and any direction you looked in, green, green, green, the whole world was moving leaves.

And under the trees the world was full of shadows. No one remembers that . . . except him, rot him.

BRICKS (*zoning out*). Boss, I really think I might . . .

SARA is edging towards PETER.

CHIPPY. Trees remember every year they've ever lived. It's written through them, it's in the wood.

PETER. It's just a tree. It's firewood.

CHIPPY. You can fell an oak tree but it'll grow again from the root.

PETER. If I fell that boy he'll stay on the ground until I put him under it. You watch.

PETER raises the axe. SARA darts at him, trying to grab the axe. He pushes her off easily, and as he does so part of his jacket tears away as if it had rotted through. Underneath he's green with leaves . . . dissolving.

SARA backs off, horrified. CHIPPY turns away at once.

BRICKS. Oh great. Now I'm hallucinating.

BRICKS passes out.

CHIPPY (*urgently*). Don't look. We're not meant to see.

PETER chops at the tree. JULIUS and JUNE hurry on. PETER whirls on them. JUNE runs forward and grabs SARA.

JUNE. Are you all right? Sara, are you . . . ?

She sees PETER's arm. She gasps and pulls SARA further back. JULIUS is taking in the whole situation: BRICKS, CHIPPY, the INDIAN BOY in the tree. He sees the axe.

Julius, his *hand*.

JULIUS (*looking*). What?

SARA (*fiercely*). Nothing. Nothing, it's just his hand. I want to go now. I want to go!

SARA *buries her head against her father.*

PETER. There's nothing for you to do here now, Julius.

JUNE *holds* SARA. JULIUS *moves to* PETER.

JUNE (*to* SARA). Don't look, I've got you. It's all right.

JULIUS. Give me the axe, Peter.

PETER. Can't do that.

JULIUS. My car's right there. I can take you and the boy back to the unit and then we can find you someone to talk to.

PETER. Oh lovely . . . nice cup of tea?

JULIUS. Yes.

PETER. Lovely. Can't happen, of course. I'd love another cup of tea. Love an early grave, actually, but you can't give me that, either. You don't know what luck is, three score years and ten of whinging about your lot . . . you want to try the alternative. I just wanted to come out into your world, Julius.

A storm starts to build, wind in the leaves. The tree sways again.

JULIUS. Peter, I can help you, just . . .

PETER (*cutting him off*). No time left.

PETER *moves for the tree,* JULIUS *pulls him back.* PETER *jerks away from him, more of his clothes disintegrate. More leaves:* PETER *is dissolving into forest.*

CHIPPY. Close your eyes and stop your ears, we're not meant to look.

SARA *is hiding her face.* JUNE *is watching.* CHIPPY *is bent over, hands over his ears.* JULIUS *can't see* PETER *at all any more.*

JULIUS. Peter? Where are you?

JUNE. He's in the tree!

PETER *starts to climb up to the* INDIAN BOY.

JULIUS. Where are you? What are you doing?

JUNE. He's going to kill the boy!

Julius, stop him!

JULIUS (*whirling, searching*). Stop what!? Where is he?

JUNE. There! In the tree!

PETER *has reached the* INDIAN BOY. *He embraces him. The* INDIAN BOY *clings to him.*

PETER. There now. It's me. I came back for you. I'll send you home.

The sound of the storm is growing.

JUNE *moves quickly to the foot of the tree.*

JUNE. Leave him!

PETER. Time to go home. Time to rest.

PETER *raises the axe.*

JUNE *yells and pushes at the tree. A flash like lightning. The tree splits and falls, burying* PETER *and the* INDIAN BOY *in a mass of leaves and branches.*

JUNE *crouches on the ground, eyes tight shut, holding her ears.*

PETER *vanishes. A roar of wind in the leaves, beating wings, swarms of insects.*

The storm dies away.

SARA *uncurls slowly.* JULIUS *and* SARA *go to* JUNE.

JUNE (*looking round, dazed*). What did I do?

JULIUS. Can you stand up?

JUNE. Where is he?

Movement in the leaves of the tree.

SARA *runs forward. She finds the* INDIAN BOY *in the wreckage of the tree. She pulls him free. She cradles him.*

SARA. It's all right. It's all right.

She holds him. The INDIAN BOY *struggles. He cries out, he wails like a very young child.*

Its all right. You're safe now. You're safe.

JULIUS *(to* JUNE). I have to see if he's all right. Just don't move . . .

JUNE *(still looking round)*. But where is he?

He quickly checks the INDIAN BOY *over, still talking to* JUNE.

CHIPPY *uncurls cautiously.*

JULIUS. You saw something. What?

JUNE. I don't know.

CHIPPY. We're not meant to know.

JULIUS *(to* CHIPPY). You saw it too?

CHIPPY. I can't remember, best we don't.

JULIUS. Sara?

SARA. I don't want to talk about it. I want to go home.

JULIUS *(to* JUNE). What was it?

JUNE. I don't know. I don't know what to tell you. I see things, Julius. You know that.

JULIUS *(indicating* CHIPPY). Yes, but he saw . . .

CHIPPY *(interrupting)*. Don't drag me into it!

JULIUS. Something happened here!

JUNE. Yes, yes it did.

SARA *(re the* INDIAN BOY). Is he all right?

JULIUS. Yes, yes, he's going to be fine. Don't worry.

SPARKS *edges out of the bushes. He's in a terrible state, mud and leaves all over him.* BRICKS *comes round.*

CHIPPY. Where were you?

SPARKS. Ditch. Has it stopped? Where is he?

CHIPPY (*sharply*). We're not asking.

    You were hiding?

SPARKS. I came back, didn't I?

BRICKS (*groggy*). My hero. Don't suppose you brought an
    ambulance?

SPARKS. They're all up there. Ambulance. Police. Can't get
    down, the road's washed out.

    JULIUS *is helping* CHIPPY *up.*

JULIUS. Can you walk?

CHIPPY (*wincing*). Yeah, yeah I'll make it.

    JULIUS *picks up the* INDIAN BOY. JUNE *guides* SARA
    after him, they exit. CHIPPY *and* SPARKS *help* BRICKS.

BRICKS. You think she'll come up the hospital, Chippy?

CHIPPY. I don't know.

BRICKS (*looking at the ground*). Are those the ones? Are
    those the feathers you were talking about? (*As* CHIPPY *is
    blank.*) Your birds! The collared whatsits with the magic
    flaming wings or whatever it . . .

CHIPPY (*getting it*). Collared doves! Yes. It's a love charm. If
    you keep the feather you'll always have true love. My
    granny told me that.

BRICKS. Well, get us a feather then!

    SPARKS *gets a feather. He gives it to* BRICKS.

    Catch me giving up the single life again.

    Still . . . can't hurt, can it?

    They move off.

INDIAN BOY'*s room. Weeks later.*

The NURSE *has had her baby. She is washing the* INDIAN
BOY / ADIL. SARA *watches.*

NURSE. There you are . . . Ajay. Nice and clean. Nice and
    warm. You're safe now.

ADIL *makes noises, pulling at her.*

What is it darling? What do you want?

ADIL *is making noises, struggling to speak. He can no longer make words, he's forgotten how to speak. He talks like a toddler.*

ADIL. Adil . . . Adil . . .

He bangs his chest, repeating.

Adil.

NURSE. Are you telling me your name, darling? Are you?

ADIL (*excited*). Adil!

NURSE. Well! Hullo Adil. Hullo.

The NURSE *beams round at* SARA.

Did you hear that? He told me his name!

ADIL. Food . . . want . . . food . . .

NURSE. Do you want a biccy? Do you? Want biccy?

ADIL.. Food . . .

NURSE. Pretty please, then . . .

ADIL. Biccy . . .

NURSE. Say please. Say please.

ADIL (*with difficulty*). Please.

NURSE. There's a good boy.

She hugs him.

You're my baby, aren't you, darling? You're my good boy.

SARA. What did you have?

NURSE. Another girl. I should've called her Storm, came in with a clap of thunder and hasn't stopped howling since.

SARA. What did you call her?

NURSE. Nicki.

She's not a good baby like my little Adil, is she, lovey?

She showers ADIL *with more kisses, gets up, big smile at* SARA.

You're not going to believe this. He's actually grown half an inch. And I had to shave him yesterday! (*Cuddling him.*) You're growing up, aren't you, Adil? Growing up at last.

The NURSE *leaves.* ADIL *looks at* SARA *and gives a huge smile.*

ADIL. Adil.

SARA. Hullo, Adil.

ADIL. Adil biccy . . .

SARA (*pointing*). Look, look out the window, Adil. Look at the tree.

ADIL *looks where she points, uncertain. He looks at the tree without interest.*

Look. It's beautiful. Look at the leaves.

ADIL *has already lost interest. He comes to* SARA *and cuddles her.* JULIUS *and* JUNE *are approaching the room, hand in hand. They stop and kiss.*

ADIL. Sara give biccy.

SARA (*stroking him*). Soon . . . soon.

JULIUS *and* JUNE *come into the room.*

JUNE. All right, sweetheart?

SARA. He's so different.

JULIUS. He's made amazing progress. Amazing. He's verbal. He's showing awareness of others. His vocabulary nearly doubles every day.

SARA. He's like a baby.

JULIUS. Yes. He's learning, like any newborn has to . . . He's learning to be part of the world again.

JUNE. You can visit him as often as you like. We thought . . . When he's more stable . . .

JULIUS. We thought we might bring him home.

JUNE. At weekends.

JULIUS. Might be therapeutic.

JUNE. He likes you.

JULIUS. What do you think?

SARA (*to* JULIUS). You're moving in again?

JULIUS. Yes.

JUNE. Are you all right with that, Sara?

SARA. If that's what's happening.

JULIUS. Yes.

SARA (*shrugs*). Fine then.

JULIUS. Your mother's going to try and manage without the pills.

JUNE. If I see things . . .

JULIUS. She's going to tell me.

JUNE. We're going to talk about it.

SARA. Do I have to talk about it?

JUNE. No.

SARA. Good.

But you're staying together. That's what's happening?

JULIUS. Yes.

JUNE. Yes.

JUNE *crouches by* ADIL, *smiling, playing with him. He plays back, grinning and gurgling.*

JULIUS. I'll be back soon. Just got to visit the wards.

JULIUS *exits.*

JUNE. You don't mind really, do you?

SARA. About what?

JUNE. If we bring him home sometimes.

SARA. I don't care. He's just a bit dull . . . that's fine. Whatever. (*Watches for a moment.*) I've decided about my subjects. I'm going to do the ones Dad can coach me in.

JUNE. All right.

SARA. You don't mind?

JUNE. No. That'd be good. For both of you.

   SARA *looks up at the tree.* JUNE *watches her.*

SARA. Did you know wolves mate for life?

   Pause.

JUNE. Well, I don't think wolves live as long as humans, do
   they?

SARA. They haven't lived here at all. Not since the trees were
   so thick you could run from one side of the country to the
   other and never get out from under the trees.

   What do you think that was like?

JUNE (*sad smile*). Dark.